"This is a wise and compassionate approach to helping couples recover from the ordinary 'stumbles' they may encounter. I think it will benefit couples who are experiencing breakdowns in communication, need to repair violations of trust, or simply recognize the wear and tear of a no-longer-brand-new relationship. I'd even recommend it as preventative work for couples who are still feeling great about their relationships."

—Dusty Miller, author of *Stop Running from Love*

"*When Love Stumbles* is a comprehensive roadmap couples in trouble can use to get their relationships back on track. I highly recommend it."

—Susan Pease Gadoua, LCSW, author of
Contemplating Divorce and *Stronger Day by Day*

when *love* stumbles

how to rediscover love, trust & fulfillment in your relationship

Randi Gunther, PhD

New Harbinger Publications, Inc.

Distributed in Canada by Raincoast Books

Copyright © 2011 by Randi Gunther
New Harbinger Publications, Inc.
5674 Shattuck Avenue
Oakland, CA 94609
www.newharbinger.com

Acquired by Melissa Kirk; Cover design by Amy Shoup;
Edited by Heather Garnos

Mixed Sources
Product group from well-managed forests and other controlled sources
www.fsc.org Cert no. SW-COC-002283
© 1996 Forest Stewardship Council

Library of Congress Cataloging-in-Publication Data

Gunther, Randi.
  When love stumbles : how to rediscover love, trust, and fulfillment in your relationship / Randi Gunther.
    p. cm.
  ISBN 978-1-57224-993-6 (pbk.) -- ISBN 978-1-57224-994-3 (pdf ebook)
  1. Couples--Psychology. 2. Interpersonal relations. 3. Man-woman relationships--Psychological aspects. 4. Love. I. Title.
  HQ801.G843 2011
  306.7--dc22

                                            2011006000

13 12 11   10 9 8 7 6 5 4 3 2 1   First printing

One of the sweetest experiences in life is to be deeply known and still beloved.

Contents

acknowledgments and gratitude

To be privileged enough to have published my first book this year, and at this point in my life, is a blessing. To have this second one following so soon afterward is an experience beyond description.

The people at New Harbinger who have made this possible are a special family of dedicated professionals who know what they are doing and are eager to help new writers. Throughout all the years of my education and supervision, I have rarely experienced the type of challenging, authentic, and accurate support they have so generously offered.

For many years, I have spent the greater part of each week deeply involved with clients I treasure, sharing significant experiences that are often life-changing. My greatest challenges and most humbling lessons have happened in those encounters. Without having known each one of them, I would not have understood the complicated processes that make intimate relationships successful.

I am deeply grateful to my husband, family, and dear friends for their enthusiastic support of my new career as an author. Though it requires my spending more time away, they willingly keep my life intact and welcome me back when a book is done.

One more. In the deepest recesses of my heart, there is the memory of a man who changed my life. He was the harshest critic I've ever known, the most brilliant therapist I've ever experienced, he was someone who believed in me when I'd lost faith in myself. Ed Jacobson died suddenly twenty-seven years ago, when he was only fifty-one. He will remain forever in my consciousness, reminding me that we are only here for a moment in time, and love is all that matters.

prologue

I remember the first time it happened. I'd been married for several years and had been up most of the night with a sick baby. I crawled into bed and looked at my husband sleeping peacefully, his out-stretched arm waiting for me.

Moonlight was shining through our window and I could see his face clearly. I felt blessed that he was there but I was aware of a strange sensation at the same time. I could take comfort in the familiarity of his face and body, but I couldn't feel his essence. It was like being in bed with an intimate stranger.

We had been so close in so many ways. Yet in that moment, I somehow knew that we had drifted apart without even realizing it. Lying quietly next to him, I also understood that we needed to find out why and do something soon to heal that separation.

I had no way of knowing then that the seemingly incongruous feeling of being so close yet so far away would happen repeatedly in the life we would lead together. I didn't realize when our love was new that no matter how committed we were to one other, our inti-mate connection would wax and wane.

I began to understand something that I wish I'd known at the beginning of our relationship. Falling in love is easy. Learning to commit more deeply when love stumbles is the greater challenge. That is the lifelong skill that partners in an intimate relationship need in order to maintain the wonderful intimacy they were able to create when their love was new.

Since then I have been married to at least twelve different men, but they are all the same person. I'm certain my husband feels that he has also had many partners. Each time we have been in danger of drifting apart, we have recommitted to being in love in a new way. To do that, we have repeatedly regenerated our relationship while simultaneously undergoing ever-new, separate personal transformations.

Now, after fifty-six years of marriage, I can openly say that our system has worked. We have had many emotional and spiritual separations, and each has brought us closer together. Through the pursuit of separate careers, years of therapy, intense searching for the wisdom of others, and the commitment to triumph over our differences, we have stayed deeply in love.

This book is the accumulation of what we have learned throughout our lives together. As I write, he stays near, working on his own newest interests, but always close at hand to share his own memories of our mutual experiences. I hope you find this process of regeneration as meaningful and as helpful as we have.

introduction

Most new lovers are highly motivated to treasure their partners. They willingly take the time to nurture each other, create pleasure, and soothe misunderstandings. In that magical process, they learn each other's languages of love, ideals, ethics, dreams, and sorrows. When misunderstandings do occur, new partners are quick to forgive each other and to learn from their mistakes.

As their relationship matures, the partners must eventually and understandably redirect their devotion and support toward other priorities. Their intense focus on each other diminishes, and their levels of availability and unconditional support decline proportionately.

Who Should Read This Book

If you are in an intimate relationship with someone you still love, but are aware that things are not as wonderful as they once were, this book will help you find the love you have lost. If you're looking for ways to regenerate the love you once knew and deeply miss, the information and exercises in this book will help you understand what may have gone wrong and guide you back to the intimacy you once shared.

How Couples Lose Their Intimate Connection

When the vitality and sweetness in a relationship diminish, it usually happens over a period of time, but the weight of a major trauma can be equally destructive. However that disintegration happens, partners often deny or bury the effects of their emotional separateness, fearing that recognizing it could threaten the relationship. They continue as if there were no significant problems, often letting unresolved issues fester, still believing that the depth of their commitment will keep their love alive.

Unfortunately, if the partners ignore too many unresolved disappointments, even what was once a very strong relationship can lose its moorings. Forgetting the exquisiteness of their original devotion, people can transform from enthusiastic lovers to exhausted strangers without realizing they are drifting apart.

Fortunately, when the partners realize there is trouble, they still have the opportunity to regenerate the deep devotion they once knew. *When Love Stumbles* will help you and your partner rediscover your capacity to love each other in those tender ways you once did. You still have within you all the skills you had when your love was new. You only need the motivation to use them again.

Guidance for Success

You will be more likely to regain what you have lost if you and your partner do the exercises in each chapter together. As you do the exercises, you are likely to uncover long-buried painful feelings that can hurt as much as they did when you first experienced them.

If you help each other recall those thoughts and feelings, you'll be closer when you've completed the exercises. If you take the time to faithfully work through the instructions, and treat each other as treasured friends in the process, you will end up remembering why you fell in love.

If your partner is not willing to participate, you will still benefit by doing the exercises independently. Try to help him or her understand that one-sided transformation can negatively affect a relationship, and that you want to heal what has been lost between you. If you are still not successful in gaining your partner's commitment, understand that you may risk a greater sense of disappointment if you grow beyond your own limitations but your partner has chosen to stay behind. If you find yourself in this position, you may want to seek the guidance of a qualified therapist.

Helpful Hints for Working Together

As you do the exercises, there are two sets of recommendations. The first set is a list of time-proven rules for good communication:

1. Use simple sentences.

2. Express your feelings without accusations.

3. Listen from your heart.

4. Don't interrupt.

5. Stay open and nondefensive.

6. Take a break if either of you feels too distressed.

7. Check in frequently with your partner to make sure he or she is on the same page, feels understood, and is open to what you have to say.

8. Stay kind.

As you open your hearts to each other again, you may feel vulnerable and exposed. The next set of recommendations will help you process any intense emotions that may come up during the exercises. Reexperiencing those feelings is a necessary step toward your ultimate success. Before each exercise, do the following:

1. Pick a time when both of you can do the exercises without feeling rushed.

2. Make sure you have the energy and motivation to put your hearts into the process.

3. Have separate journals handy. You will be asked to use them in many of the exercises.

4. Select a comfortable place free from interruption and safe for both of you.

5. Take a few moments to become centered before each interaction.

6. Be prepared to hear your partner's thoughts and feelings without judgment.

7. Be ready to share any of your own thoughts or feelings that would help your partner to better understand your needs.

8. Ask for each other's support and understanding.

9. When you are both ready, fully engage in the current exercise.

10. When both of you have completed your assignment, alternately share what you have written.

11. Ask your partner what he or she feels and thinks about what you have shared. Do not disagree, defend, or invalidate. Just thank him or her for sharing.

12. Take a few moments to relax together and to allow your feelings to calm down.

13. Encourage each other to keep working together on the exercises that follow.

If you feel overwhelmed at any time, ask your partner to wait with you while you regain your composure. Holding hands during this time can be helpful. Any amount of encouragement or comfort you can extend to your partner throughout the exercises will help.

Return to these helpful hints throughout the next chapters and the exercises within them. They will help reinforce what you are learning.

Readiness Evaluation

To explore whether you are ready to work on healing your relationship, you and your partner should each answer the following questions privately before you share them with each other. It will help to write your answers down in your separate journals.

When you have written all your responses, share each one in turn. As your partner tells you his or her answers, jot them down next to yours so that you can compare them. Taken together, they will help you see how close you still are or how far you may have drifted from your original commitment to each other. The answers will be an important foundation for later exercises.

Score each answer from 1 to 5 using the following criteria. Make a separate total score for each of you and then add your scores together:

Very rarely = 1

Occasionally = 2

More often than not = 3

Often = 4

Almost always = 5

1. When you think back to the beginning of your relationship, do you still have sweet memories and nostalgic feelings?

2. Are there moments when you look at your partner and feel grateful that he or she is still part of your life?

3. When you think back to the beginning of your relationship, are you still able to get in touch with the love you felt then?

4. Are there still moments where you remember why you chose your partner?

5. Do you still respect and treasure your partner even when you are angry or hurt?

6. If you get away together and leave current pressures behind, do you still enjoy each other's company?

7. When someone else is interested in your partner, do you feel proud that he or she is committed to you?

8. When you feel positive emotions toward your partner, are you likely to express them?

The higher your total score, the more you have held on to the intimacy you felt when your love was new. The lower your total score, the less you may feel committed and hopeful about your intimacy with your partner.

No matter what your own score is, your partner's score also counts in predicting how well your relationship will heal. A combined score of 50 or more would indicate a very positive outcome. A score below 30 will mean that you both will have to work much harder to regain what you've lost. It may take more time and effort, but as long as you both believe that your relationship is healable, you can make it happen.

It's much easier to keep up your momentum if you feel an equal part of the same team, but do not be discouraged if your totals are not as close as you would have hoped. It is possible that one of you may have to put out more energy at the beginning, but those efforts will even out by the time you have gone through all of the exercises together.

Your success will depend on your level of commitment. You can view your disappointments and disillusionments as barriers to love or as welcome opportunities for healing. If you are committed to the process, those barriers will diminish as you go through the steps to revitalize your relationship.

How to Use This Book

Chapter 1 reviews the eight most common ways your love may have stumbled. You may find that any or all of them may apply to your relationship. If there are other stumbles that are more personal to your partnership, the six steps in chapter 2 will let you work on any that are not explored here. Chapters 3 through 10 examine each of the eight stumbles in detail, with specific exercises for you and your partner to do together. Chapter 11 identifies the conscious and unconscious warning signs that will help you recognize when a stumble is happening.

There may be times when you and your partner are both making enthusiastic and heartfelt efforts to find your way back to each other, but feel frustrated that you are not making enough progress. If you feel that you are floundering despite your genuine commitment to revitalize your relationship, don't feel you have failed. It may be time to find a competent therapist to help objectively guide you toward a more successful outcome.

1

discovering the stumbles

When Sara and Ben came into my office for counseling, they were disillusioned and emotionally exhausted. After doing everything they could to regenerate their love for each other, they had been unable to feel hopeful about a future together.

Ben started. "We've read every self-help book on the market, been to couples retreats, planned romantic weekends—you know, everything you're supposed to do to make things better. We still can't seem to stop fighting over stupid things and blaming each other. We know we're killing the love between us, but we can't stop. I don't know about Sara, but I'm damn embarrassed to be here, asking some guru to point out stuff I can't see."

Sara agreed, looking nervously at Ben. "I feel the same way Ben does." She smiled sadly. "It's probably the first thing we've agreed on in months. We don't want to give up, but we really don't know what else to do."

They described themselves as angry strangers, interacting with bitterness and irritation, stuck in self-righteousness and stubbornness. They could not share thoughts without arguing or allow themselves to be vulnerable enough to make love. Facing the threat of separation, they had come to counseling as their last resort.

"How do your disagreements start, and what precedes them?" I asked.

"She picks on everything goddamned thing I do," Ben said. "I can't walk across a room without her telling me I'm going in the wrong direction."

"He's so exaggerating," Sara interrupted. "Just to make me look bad. I only correct him when he's about to do something stupid. I'm just trying to help and he knows that. I could say things in the kindest way possible and he'd still think I'm some kind of witch-bitch. He hates me."

"Sure, sure. There you go. Make it all my fault, like I'm crazy or something."

I interrupted. "Can you let me help you look at this from a different point of view?"

Ben shrugged. Sara could not meet my eyes, but was quiet.

"I'm assuming that you got along well enough at one point to make a lifetime commitment to each other. When did these problems begin to surface?"

"Probably about our third year together, after our trip to Europe." Sara looked at Ben. He nodded.

"Did you fight like this when your love was new?"

"Of course not," Ben said. "She loved everything about me. I couldn't do anything wrong. Just being near her felt like I had found the home I never had."

Sara looked at Ben, then began to cry. "But you *were* perfect. I lived for the moments you would come home. You listened to every detail of my day as if I were the most important thing in your world."

Ben turned away, wiping his eyes.

I asked them both, "When did you become aware that things were not the same?"

"You go first, Ben," Sara said, aware of his vulnerability.

He collected himself. "It's hard to pinpoint any specific event. We just started to pick on each other for little things. Each one seems so stupid in retrospect, but, at the time, they got to me."

"Can you give Sara an example?"

"Let me think. Yeah. It was Christmas morning, the day after our third anniversary. After we woke up and made love, I was totally open. I was remembering some painful things that happened to me when I was a kid that I finally felt I could talk about.

"Then the phone rang. It was Sara's mother. They talked for over an hour. I got pissed waiting to talk to her, and finally got up to take a shower. I know I was a bear for the rest of the day and Sara was clueless."

Sara looked surprised. "But we talked about going for a bike ride. Mom and I were just talking about recipes. Nothing important. I didn't know you wanted to talk, Ben. Why didn't you say something?"

"And stop you from doing what you obviously preferred? No chance."

"But I would have loved to hear what you had to say. I didn't even know why you were so irritable all day. That wasn't fair."

They looked at me, lost again.

"How would that scenario have been different when you were first in love? What would have happened?" I asked.

They looked into each other's eyes.

Sara smiled. "Ben would have held on to me when the phone rang, like he used to. He'd be teasing me while I was talking, and I'd want to get off the phone and go back to being with him. I would have known we weren't through and I'd have told my mom I'd call her back later."

"Do you remember when things changed?"

She thought about it for a moment. "No, not really. It seemed to happen slowly."

Ben nodded.

I began to understand. "It sounds as if you've gradually become more upset with each other in many ways. Did either of you notice that you were drifting apart?"

Ben responded. "When we were first together, we always made each other the top priority. We never hurt each other this way. All I cared about was making her happy. How did we get here?" He reached for Sara's hand.

Where Did Their Relationship Stumble?

Watching Ben and Sara open up to each other again, I understood something so basic and relevant that I wondered how I'd missed it before.

This couple still loved each other as much as they always had, but that love was buried under layers of misunderstandings and disappointments. They hadn't forgotten how to love, *they had lost the motivation to love.* They didn't need to be taught new skills; they needed to find out why they had stopped using the skills they already had.

The crucial questions were obvious to us:

- Why did they let their love diminish?

- How could such well-meaning partners justify withholding their once-tender thoughts and feelings?

- When and how did their desire to express those kindnesses fall away?

- Were they aware of the extent to which their emotional connection was diminishing?

There were obviously layers of anger and blame to be dealt with, but their underlying love had survived despite those factors. If they could understand how they had lost each other, they could find their way back.

A *Plan of Hope*

Ben and Sara's destructive patterns were not insurmountable, but their defenses and righteous positions had become entrenched. They hadn't even endured the most common tragedies that often drive couples apart, and they had started out deeply in love. There had been no infidelity, no major losses, and no debilitating stressors in their years together, yet their relationship was dying.

Setting up a plan of hope early in therapy is crucial, and this couple desperately needed it. Despite the layers of desperation and despair, they had come for help.

Over the next few sessions, we carefully explored how and when Ben and Sara had gone from positive feelings toward each other to negative patterns and diminished motivation. Eventually, we were able to identify those events that were the most crucial. Together, we labeled them "stumbles," places where their devotion had drifted and had not been recovered.

From that awareness, they could pinpoint when they had begun losing each other. They began to wonder: if they had been able to recognize those moments, situations, or sequences at the time, could they have done something to resolve them? And now, if they could retrieve their early moments of treasuring each other, would that help them heal?

Together, we decided how best to make that happen. As they remembered when and how their stumbles began, and what they might have done differently, they created a second chance. The love they feared lost resurfaced, inspiring them to work even harder on the relationship they both wanted.

I have now shared this process with hundreds of couples. With their combined input, I have reworked and refined the most common stumbles, and I've created a six-step healing plan that will help you and your partner identify where you stand on each of these continuums. Working the steps together, you can learn how to reclaim what you have lost and find your love again.

The Most Common Stumbles

The rest of this chapter will describe the eight most common stumbles. Though they overlap in some ways, they also have characteristics that are very different. Taken together, they capture the essence of how couples lose their intimacy. After each stumble is described, there will be some questions to help you decide whether this stumble feels familiar. The questions will guide you in discussing its special importance to you and your partner.

Chapter 2 will describe the steps of a healing plan that applies universally to any relationship stumble. You can practice it with the eight common stumbles, but it is also applicable to any stumble not described in this book. Chapters 3 through 10 will explore each of the stumbles in more detail and will offer specific exercises to help you and your partner find your way back to each other. Chapter 11 will help you identify the conscious and unconscious emotional symptoms that signal a stumble in process.

From Fulfillment to Disillusionment

"You don't seem to care the way you used to."

Lovers in new relationships are exquisitely available to each other. They are spontaneously generous, trusting, and considerate. Armed with intimacy radar, they anticipate each other's needs and delight in meeting them before they are asked. As the relationship matures, the partners often become less motivated and less generous than they once were. Understandable disillusionments accumulate, and the time and energy required to fulfill their partner's needs can become more burdensome.

To avoid recognizing the situation, many partners dull out the awareness of their diminished caring, deliberately or absentmindedly disregarding the signals they would have responded to in the past. They rationalize that their rearrangements in priorities are understandable and shouldn't affect the core of their love.

Ben and Sara fell prey to the same lack of awareness. As their unfulfilled desires increased, they stopped asking for what they wanted and allowed their cumulative misunderstandings to become an emotional barrier between them.

To check how far your relationship may have drifted from fulfillment to disappointment, consider the following questions:

1. When you want something special, does your partner sense it without your having to ask?

2. Have you scaled back your desires so that you are less likely to be disappointed?

3. Do you feel irritated when you know your partner wants something and you don't feel like offering it?

4. Do you wonder what happened to the partner who seemed to know what you needed and always came through?

5. Do you still enjoy doing something sweet for your partner that he or she doesn't expect?

From Excitement to Boredom

"What happened to our spark?"

Excitement is the natural response to novelty, discovery, and challenge. Most new relationships have those experiences in abundance. We are hunters by nature, and the pursuit of a new love brings out the thrill of the chase and the acquisition of the prize.

Sadly, over time, most partners do not put the same energy into maintenance as they did into the hunt. They opt instead for familiarity and comfort, and they stop seeking the emerging discoveries that keep new lovers so emotionally alive. "Same old, same old" is the formula for boredom, and boredom is the breeding ground for discontent and alienation.

When couples choose security over excitement too much of the time, passion will eventually diminish in any relationship. Without the energy that challenges create, comfort will predominate, and the partners will accept the compromises they have created, losing the magnetic thrill they once had.

To check how far your relationship may have drifted from excitement to boredom, consider the following questions:

1. When you're out with your partner alone, do you wish you felt more alive?

2. Has your relationship become less exciting because of too many predictable habits?

3. Does your mind wander when your partner is talking to you?

4. Do you feel irritated or bored but are unable to tell your partner how you are feeling?

5. Does it take less and less energy to run your relationship?

6. When either of you feels bored, do you pick fights just to stir things up?

From Constructive Challenges to Destructive Conflicts

"Why does every disagreement become an argument?"

New lovers are genuinely interested in what their partners know, wonder about, believe in, and pursue. They listen deeply, ask each other questions, and compare answers and opinions. Though they may be looking for experiences they can share, they treasure their curiosity more than automatic agreement.

Differences rarely become deal breakers when love is new. Good debates are mutually satisfying searches for common truths, and they deepen the commitment to the relationship as the participants support, validate, and share their worldviews.

Unfortunately, as time passes, many couples begin seeing those once pleasurable differences as barriers to comfort. What once were spirited debates now become arguments for control. If those interactions become consistently competitive and oppositional, the partners become adversaries, forgetting they were once on the same team.

To check how far your relationship may have drifted from exploring differences to destructive conflicts, consider the following questions:

1. When you and your partner don't see eye to eye on something, do you quickly become adversaries?

2. When differing, do you move rapidly from inquiry to judgment to volatility?

3. Have you stopped listening to your partner's point of view if it doesn't coincide with your own?

4. Do you feel as if your partner puts you down when you try to talk about what you think?

5. Does either of you feel you will be ignored or drowned out if you don't convince your partner to think as you do?

From Sacrificing for Your Partner to Self-Preservation

"I can't always put you first anymore."

New lovers trust each other's intentions and availability. They willingly share their resources and trust they will be treated in kind. Sacrificing for the other seems natural, and new partners are more likely to give love in abundance without concern for reciprocity.

As relationships mature, the partners may find themselves less willing to automatically be generous with one another. What once was a mutual psychological bank account with heavy assets now seems drained and in debt. Each partner becomes more self-preserving at the cost of the other's needs.

To see how far your relationship may have drifted from putting your partner first to choosing self-preservation, consider the following questions:

1. Are you confident your partner would sacrifice for you if it were something important?

2. Does either one of you feeling more entitled to receive than give?

3. Are you less likely to sacrifice for your partner, even for an appropriate request?

4. Do you find yourself prioritizing your own needs even when you know your partner would rather you focus on him or her?

5. Have you stopped asking permission?

6. Do you feel less responsible for your partner's well-being than you did when your relationship was new?

From Being a Team to Operating Solo

"We used to do everything together. Now I handle most of my challenges without you."

In the early stages of a love relationship, new lovers respond enthusiastically and supportively to each other's problems. The result is instant teamwork. When two people combine their resources with love and cooperation, distresses are lessened and joys are increased. Both partners are available whenever needed and will fight for each other in the world.

When relationship stressors cause partners to drift apart, the partners also stop working as a team. They begin to solve their problems separately just to avoid any conflict that might arise. Sadly, as they become less available to each other, they fear being let down or invalidated if they ask for help. The relationship goes from intertwined team members to parallel problem solvers with diminished communication and less intimacy.

To see how far your relationship may have drifted from being a team to operating alone, consider the following questions:

1. When you ask your partner for help, is he or she less motivated to respond to your request than before?

2. Are you spending more time relying on your own resources rather than risking rejection from your partner?

3. When you ask for emotional or physical support, do you expect to be dismissed rather than supported?

4. Do you feel a pre-defeat before you reach out for help, as if your partner is simply not motivated to work with you anymore?

5. Has it become easier just to solve your own problems rather than to try to get support and energy from your partner?

From Feeling Unconditionally Loved to Being on Trial

"Before, you loved me without question. Now I have to fight to prove my worth."

The automatic bestowals of love and acceptance between new intimate partners are similar to those that exist between most parents and their children. Cherishing is automatic and burdens are willingly accepted. Bathing in that unconditional love, new partners do the same. They focus intensely on what they love about each other and do not allow themselves to pay attention to existing or potential defects.

Used to that wondrous level of security, committed lovers feel their partners are being unfair of they withhold that comfort. The lover they once knew no longer automatically accepts every truth as valid and every behavior as well-intentioned. Behaviors that were acceptable when love was new must now be justified before support is available.

To see how far your relationship may have drifted from your safe havens, consider the following questions:

1. Do you feel you often have to convince your partner that your desires are legitimate when you need something?

2. Do you feel guilty and embarrassed when you do something your partner criticizes?

3. Do you feel trepidation when you have to tell your partner something that might be upsetting?

4. Are you quick to defend when your partner questions something you are doing?

5. Does your partner make you feel like you need to justify your requests for support?

From Focusing on the Relationship to Pursuing Outside Interests

"I know I'm gone a lot, but I need more stimulation."

New lovers only have eyes for each other. The timeless joy of sharing and exploring their emotional, spiritual, intellectual, sexual, and physical worlds seems endless and captivating. The rest of life becomes a blur as they focus intently on each other. Their love is all they need to feel complete.

As their partnership becomes more established, one or both partners may not feel as completely fulfilled by the relationship alone and will seek outside stimulation to meet those needs. At first, those alternative outlets may not be threatening. Some of them may even bring new energy into the relationship and help the lovers to rediscover each other, but others may take their energy away from the primary relationship, diminishing its vitality.

Partners who fulfill most of their interests outside the relationship are always in danger of comparing the more novel experience to the one at home. If that happens, they may find themselves magnifying dissatisfactions and justifying more time away.

To see how your need for stimulation has drifted from your relationship to outside interests, consider the following questions:

1. When you return from new experiences, do you feel closer to your partner or less intimate?

2. Do you miss each other when you're away and look forward to seeing each other when you return?

3. Are you actively seeking ways to spend more time away from the relationship?

4. When you are together, do you find yourself wishing you were somewhere else, doing something different?

5. Do you feel that you can't seem to create novelty or new challenges in your relationship?

From Common Goals to Different Dreams

"We just don't want the same things anymore."

Whether it be a devotion to the same spiritual or philosophical beliefs or a love of hugging trees, all couples need to share something that is beyond their devotion to each other. In times of trouble, that common faith or value strengthens the commitment and increases the motivation to stay together.

Having similar spiritual, intellectual, and emotional direction helps a couple recommit to each other when they face hard times. Sharing faith, partners are able to remind each other of the beauty they have created together, and they can recommit to the reasons they chose each other.

In the beginning of a relationship, most couples strive to define and honor what they believe in together and what it will take to make their dreams come true. They revisit those sacred beliefs as often as needed to maintain the freshness and passion of their mutual faith. If that common bond weakens, once-loving partners can drift away from their potential for regeneration.

To see how far your relationship may have drifted from your devotion to mutual sacred beliefs, consider the following questions:

1. When was the last time you sat down together and thought about the blessings of your relationship?

2. Do you still believe in the sacredness of your love?

3. How far have you strayed from what is most important to both of you, and in what ways?

4. Do you return to your spiritual/psychological beliefs when the relationship is stressed?

5. Has either of you adopted a different set of values without including your partner?

Assessing Your Stumbles

As you read through the eight most common stumbles, you will find that some have more relevance to you than others. They may have been noticeable early in your relationship or may have taken months or years to emerge. Each one can affect any other and they can happen separately or in concert. Healing one can result in the healing of any other.

Early intervention can prevent a stumble from developing, keep it from generating other stumbles, and help it get better if it has begun. For example, partners who renew their excitement for each other, or maintain their loving support, are much more likely to begin working as a team again.

As you assess these stumbles together, pick those that are most significant to each of you. Because the exercises are challenging and may bring up difficult emotions, you may want to first work on one that is not as problematic.

The next chapter will outline the steps of your healing plan. Doing the exercises throughout the book will give you the tools to find your way back to the love you once knew.

the healing plan

Every committed relationship is vulnerable to stumbling. No matter how much we initially promise to treasure each other forever, we are all susceptible to forgetting the sacredness of those commitments. The automatic devotion that once seemed so impervious to erosion can innocently diminish through neglect.

For whatever reasons you have drifted from the more loving couple you once were, you can find that love again. Understanding how you got to where you are now is crucial to building a renewed commitment—one that will bring you back home to the love you've known.

This chapter's healing plan will give you the six steps you'll need to help you with any personal stumbles that may currently exist in your relationship. In each succeeding chapter, you'll be given specific exercises that apply to each individual stumble. You can read them separately or in sequence.

Assuring a Successful Outcome

Because the exercises are meant to be penetrating and meaningful, I recommend that you embrace them with a positive and supportive attitude. They are designed to reach deeply into your past and to create new options for the future. This is the only way to help you change your future together. Going through the exercises often brings emotions to the surface that you may have pushed aside. Give yourselves enough room in your schedules to do the exercises on a regular basis and be sure to allow yourselves adequate, uninterrupted time to process your experience.

You can choose to do several of the exercises at the same time if you can stay calm and connected, but if either of you becomes too emotional to successfully continue, let things quiet down before committing to the next step.

It may take a while to evaluate your feelings and to openly share your deepest truths. Make certain your partner can reflect back to you what he or she understood you to say. Take whatever time you need to resolve any misunderstandings before continuing. Go at your own pace, and make certain you maintain respect and compassion for each other along the way. I will remind you of these attitudes and behaviors continually throughout the book, because they are crucial to your success.

Step One: Go Back to the Beginning of Your Relationship

Your first step is to revisit how you felt when you were newly in love. Each chapter will ask you to remember those exceptional moments when you were captivated by each other. You'll re-create the experiences and feelings that intrigued you and the behaviors you found so delicious. Try to recall times that were important and memorable— those that were the most tender and sweet and made you choose each other over everyone else. The sweeter the memory, the more successful the exercise will be.

Though you might think otherwise, this first step is often uncomfortable for many couples. Because your love has stumbled, you may have erected boundaries to keep your partner from knowing when you're vulnerable. It's sometimes painful to bring those protective walls down.

Here is an example of the kind of story you might share with your partner in the first step of the healing process. You can choose to write it down and let your partner read it on his or her own, or you can read it aloud so that you can be certain your partner will hear the emotions that you are feeling.

Example

"I was thirty-one years old when I met you. I'd gone through a dozen or so relationships that all seemed okay at the beginning but never lasted very long. I'd begun to think I was too jaded or too stupid to choose well, and I was about ready to give up.

"It was one of those late nights when I just couldn't get to sleep. I'll never know what made me suddenly hungry enough to brave the weather and go to Denny's, but thank God I did.

"I was at my table reading as usual, and I didn't look up right away when you came to take my order. When I did, I swore I had seen the face of an angel. I'd never seen such beautiful blue eyes. I couldn't speak. Remember?

"You blushed and I sneezed. We both laughed. You asked me what I would like. In my head, I answered, 'To spend the rest of my life with you,' but managed to get out something about coffee and a bagel.

"When you came back, I couldn't hold my feelings in any longer, and I asked you if you would have coffee with me after your shift. I remember your facial expression so well. You were obviously trying to decide if I was crazy. You asked for a few moments to think about it and went to put in my order. When you came back and said yes, I knew my life would change forever."

Suggestions

The example in this section and those in the rest of the book were chosen from actual experiences. The sharing may seem unusually revealing and vulnerable. Please don't expect to share your thoughts and feelings easily when you first begin doing the exercises.

After a while, though, you will find yourself able to communicate with your partner in a wonderfully natural and intimate way.

Step Two: Evaluate Your Current Relationship

Before you can use the past to create a new future, you'll need to examine what you are feeling toward your partner in the present. Knowing how far you've drifted from your original feelings will give you a reality check on what you need to change.

Your goal in carefully observing the present is to uncover any underlying feelings that could keep you from moving ahead. Like many of us, you may have been taught that if you truly love someone, you should not be harboring feelings of martyrdom, chronic resentment, or wishes for retaliation. If you believe those negative feelings are undesirable, you may have buried them and turned them into chronic bitching, whining, nagging, complaining, blaming, withholding, defensiveness, patronizing statements, or contempt.

Whatever negative feelings you may be harboring, you have enough positives in your relationship to still love each other. Perhaps you've made unconscious or conscious compromises, or tried to focus on what you still value, but you may just be protecting your vulnerability behind those emotional curtains. You may think that you were supposed to stay madly in love forever, and feeling less passionate means you have failed.

Regardless of how you came to feel this way, your new goal is to honestly bring each other up to date on what you are feeling now. Be certain to let your partner know the positives you still feel exist in the relationship as well as the negatives. Admit whatever you feel your own contributions are, and avoid blaming your partner. If both partners' feelings and thoughts feel welcomed and not judged, you will learn much more about each other.

Using the following questions as a guide, compose a narrative to your partner that describes how you are feeling in the present. Use only the questions that are helpful, and add your own if they are more pertinent. Be as honest as you can with yourself before you share your thoughts with your partner. Use however many words you need to help him or her understand. You may wish to write your narrative in your journal first, in order to make certain you are comfortable with what you want to say before sharing it.

- How do I withhold my love from you even when I feel it?

- When I act in a negative or hurtful manner toward you, what am I truly feeling that I'm not sharing?

- What are the positive things I still feel about you?

- When I invalidate the things you do or say, why am I doing that?

- How have I become hard to live with?

- How am I staying emotionally armored with you?

- In what ways have I changed that have turned you away?

- What do I most resent about our relationship?

- What do I most miss about the relationship we used to have?

- What do I still look forward to or enjoy doing with you?

- What would I miss if we were not together anymore?

- What do you do or say that hurts me the most?

- When do I feel the most forgiving?

- How hopeful am I that we can change?

- Do I believe that you still love me enough to try to heal our relationship?

Example

"Sometimes, when we're with other people, I hear your laughter from the other side of the room and my heart feels heavy. I've always loved hearing you laugh, but I hold back from telling you now. Instead I pick on the things that I know will make you feel insecure. I can hear myself pointing out that extra five pounds and giving you a hard time when you order dessert, but in reality, I'm still turned on by you as much as ever. I guess I just don't want you to take me for granted.

"I don't say the things that I know would make you happy because I feel too inadequate to give you enough to make a difference. I think I resent feeling responsible for you.

"I've given up trying to talk to you about things that are important to me, because you usually redirect the conversation to other topics or start talking about your feelings again. Sometimes I wish you'd just listen and not try to change me.

"I've never been unfaithful or given you any reason to doubt me, but you get really upset when I talk to other women and constantly ask me if I'm going to stick around. I get tired of trying to prove myself to you. I want you to feel secure with me, but I'm tired of constantly reassuring you. Deep inside, you mean the world to me, but I don't want to be rejected if I reach out to you. I'd be willing to do anything to fall in love with you again."

Example

"When I would come into a room, your eyes would light up. You'd walk across the room to hug me no matter who else was watching. You seemed so proud of me, like you were the luckiest guy on earth.

"Now, you hardly seem to notice I'm there. Every time I ask you to do something for me, you act like it's a burden. If I only talk about what is important to you, then you'll give me a little more time, but if I waver, you drift off and seem uninterested.

"I know I still love you, but I miss the affection you used to give me. Now it's only when you want sex and then it's over. We used to do everything together. Now you stay late at work or want to play golf or go to a hockey game with your friends. I know you're not the type to have an affair, but it would almost be easier if there were someone else. At least your lack of interest in me would make more sense.

"You tell me you still love me, but you don't show it the way you used to. I try to do everything you love, but it doesn't seem to make a difference anymore. When I ask you what I could do instead, you seem irritated and say that things are fine, even when we both know they're not. There was a time when I couldn't imagine my life without you, but now I'm not so sure.

"Maybe I'm just holding on to a memory that only exists in my own mind. I know I would miss your sense of humor and the way you touch me when you want to be close. And the way you are with my family, so kind and available. Sometimes we laugh like we used to and everything seems okay. But it doesn't last. I'm so unhappy. It's like I'm the only one fighting for this relationship."

Suggestions

When the time comes to share, you may feel some trepidation and wonder how your partner will receive what you have to say. Sometimes it is easier to start with letting your partner read what you wrote first so he or she can digest it more slowly.

When you share your responses with your partner, you may find yourselves talking in new ways, and you may feel emotions you didn't expect. Refer back to the helpful hints in the introduction to make certain you keep your communication open and supportive.

Step Three: When Did You Begin to Drift?

Stumbles can happen suddenly from an unexpected crisis, but they usually start slowly and go unnoticed for a long time. Most couples choose to ignore the small distresses that often fall under the radar. They would rather continue interacting as they are and focus on the positives of their relationship.

In this step, you'll learn how recalling those smaller disconnects that went unattended will help you heal and prevent new stumbles from forming. In the subsequent chapters, you'll use such recollections to identify when specific feelings began to develop that contributed to the stumble you are exploring.

Use the following questions to begin your preparation. It may be helpful to answer them privately before you begin your exercises. You can write your feelings and thoughts in your journal so you can refer to them later.

It is not important that your answers be perfectly formed or accurate. Right now, you are just beginning to explore your feelings. Give yourself the freedom to simply reminisce without judgment.

- Do you remember a time or event that made you feel as if you and your partner were drifting apart?

- Did you believe that your relationship was in trouble when those experiences occurred?

- What stopped you from resolving what was going on at the time?

- What else was happening that might have kept you from reaching out?

Your goal is to help each other recall when those hurtful or disappointing experiences first began happening. Try to remember when your hurt lasted a little too long or when pride became a barrier that kept you from each other.

Example

"I remember the night when that drunk woman at the party came on to me. Sure, I was pretty buzzed, but I could have stopped it if I'd cared. I guess I was still pissed from our last fight. It put me over the edge. I couldn't keep trying to give you what you wanted and listen to your constant nagging about my unavailability at the same time. When we left for the party, I think I was angry in a different way than ever before.

"You did try to make up to me in the car like you've always done, making small talk about what our friends would do when we arrived, even patting my leg like you wanted me to pretend that nothing was wrong. But something had changed and I couldn't look at you. Inside I still wanted to reach out and make everything okay, but I was too fed up and I didn't want to reward you for the way you acted.

"I'll never forget the look on your face when you saw me kissing her in the hallway. I never intended to take it further, but I knew I'd crossed the line. I wasn't surprised when you called a cab and went home without me.

"I knew we needed to talk, but I just couldn't deal with another tirade. I was out of motivation and new ideas. I left the party right after you did, but stayed at my friend's place that night so you would think I was with her. I wanted to hurt you the way you'd been hurting me for months. Maybe that wasn't fair, and it certainly didn't help the situation, but I didn't want to care anymore.

"We didn't speak for two weeks, and then we never brought it up again. I don't think our relationship has ever fully recovered, and I wish I'd talked to you about this sooner and tried to work it out."

Suggestions

When you reveal embarrassing or painful experiences from the past, you may feel exposed and fearful of your partner's response. He or she may be familiar with some of the memories, but others may be new or surprising. That is why it is so important to do these exercises when both of you have the time and energy to put your heart into the process, and to continuously commit to your mutual support and validation.

The goal is to deeply understand each other, not to use old hurts to get back at your partner. Remind each other that you are in this for the long haul. The way you care for each other when you do these exercises will predict your success in the future.

Step Four: What Prevented Your Recovery at the Time This Stumble Occurred?

It is highly probable that whatever stopped you from healing those disconnects in the past may still be operating in your current relationship. Paying attention to what made you ignore them before may help you identify them now.

Bringing back negative experiences is hard for anyone. It is embarrassing to relive what you did wrong, especially when you realize how much your relationship has suffered because of those choices. Even so, you must try to let your vulnerability return, or risk missing those same cues again.

You can't go back and change what has already happened, but it's easier to forgive each other if you can believe in a different future. Hopefully, in doing the first three steps, you will have recognized when you become defensive. Try to keep in mind your common goals when those responses threaten to surface. If you are having trouble staying calm and open, tell your partner you are feeling overwhelmed, and ask for support and some time to regain your composure.

Before you begin the exercise in this step, promise yourself that you will listen deeply to your partner's honest responses, and maintain a welcome attitude toward whatever is shared, even if you do not agree. Your goal will be to keep your partner feeling open, safe, and unafraid of your condemnation.

You most certainly won't agree with all that you hear, nor do you need to. Everyone remembers the past differently, and usually in a self-preserving manner. Assume that all your partner's feelings are justified, even if the reasons he or she gives for them may not seem valid. In advance, plan to support and validate your partner's memories, even if you feel unfairly accused or inaccurately represented. The greatest gift you can give your partner is your support.

It is only when you can approach each other with that level of acceptance that true healing can begin. Your goal in going into the past is to keep those barriers from reforming in the present. The more you are willing to risk in reliving your thoughts and emotions, the more you will learn. Silence and withholding are the enemies of intimacy.

Most partners want the best for each other and do not want their intimacy to diminish. Yet, situations happen that keep them from resolving their stumbles before they become entrenched.

The goal of this step is to understand why you may have looked away when your relationship began to drift. Use the following examples from others who have done the exercises in the book. Their examples will help guide you. Read through the list and see if you recognize any of these feelings in yourself or your partner, and add those that are personal to you. Please do not negatively judge yourself or wish you had been different. Again, learning about the past will help you identify stumbles in the future.

When you have identified your own feelings, write them into a narrative that you will share with your partner.

- I was too angry to ask you for anything. I figured you would come to me when you were ready.

- I thought you'd never get past what I did, so I didn't try to fix it.

- I was afraid to be vulnerable with you because I expected you to hurt me again.

- I wanted to tell you what was going on with me, but I didn't trust your response.

- I didn't want you to get angrier, so I just accepted what was going on and hoped it would get better.

- I was so discouraged by what had happened that I wanted to hurt you back by not letting you make things better.

- I thought you'd just think I was being stupid and making too much of things, so I gave up and didn't try.

- I was sorry I did what I did, but I knew you'd never let it go, so I just shut up and hoped it would go away.

- I thought talking about it would just make it worse.

- I wanted you but I wasn't willing to go through your hoops to get out of the doghouse.

Example

"I knew we were drifting apart, but I thought I was the only one who was feeling it. I never know how to approach you, because I anticipate that you'll twist my words and accuse me of putting you down and justifying getting more distant. I could never figure out what was going on in your head.

"I feel stupid about admitting this, but sometimes I didn't push it because I wanted to see if you'd get it on your own. I knew I could count on your reaching out when you finally needed something from me, and by that time, I was feeling lonely enough to reconnect, but some part of me wasn't buying it in the same way anymore.

"I'd fantasize about having a relationship with someone else, but in some weird way, my thoughts always triggered your radar. Out of nowhere you'd want me again. I never could resist, but I'd feel like a fool, giving in like that without telling you what I was feeling. I guess I just couldn't handle the hassle and hoped things would be better.

"I didn't realize I still had so much anger in me, but getting it out feels better. I hope you can hear me this time without making it about you. I'm not trying to make this all your fault and I'm willing to do whatever I can to turn this around."

Suggestions

When you do these exercises together, this step may take many tries before both of you feel that you've gotten to the bottom of the stumble. Unexpected emotions often arise. If they do, practice what you have prepared to do, staying open and nonjudgmental. If things become too hard, remember to take a break and do something rewarding together for a while.

Don't move on to the next step until you feel centered again. You can repeat this step as often as you need to, provided that it continues to help you share openly without conflict.

Step Five: What Do You Need from Each Other Now to Reawaken Your Love?

Hopefully, when you get to this point in each chapter, you will have:

- Remembered how well you loved each other when you were newly together

- Compared those feelings and actions with where you are today

- Helped one another remember how you drifted off course

With those memories close at hand, you'll be on your way to recapturing what you once had. Unresolved emotional scars can doom a relationship that cannot grow beyond them, but new awareness and renewed commitments can change those limitations and take you beyond those barriers.

Here are some examples of what others have said when they've completed this step. These statements are only meant to be guidelines, but they can give you a preview of what is possible. You are free to create additional examples for yourselves:

- I want you to forgive me for the things I've said and done that have hurt you.

- I want you to tell me what are the most important things you need from me now.

- I need to know that you will help me to feel safe and beloved in your presence again.

- I want you to encourage me in the places I'm frightened, and respect my choices when I need to find my own way.

- I'm willing to do whatever I can to help you pull down the barriers between us.

- I want to let you back into my heart and trust that you will not hurt me again.

- I want us to respect our differences and strive to include them in our lives.

Example

"This is hard for me, but I want to do what's right for us, and I need your help. I've loved you so much for so long, and I know those feelings are still inside. I've buried them under words I shouldn't have said or those I didn't have the courage to say. I can't imagine my life without you, and I want to love you the way you deserve to be loved. I want to feel your body against me again, open and safe.

"I realize that your forgiveness can only happen over time, and only if you believe things will be different. I don't expect that to happen overnight, but I need to know when I'm on the right track, and to believe that you are as eager to make this work as I am.

"Please help me succeed. I'll need reminders and encouragement from you. Don't save up your anger or surprise me with something I did wrong that you were afraid to tell me about. I'd rather have it up front and deal with it right away.

"I want us to love each other openly the way we once did, and I'll do everything I can to make that happen."

After you've shared these desires with each other, you will feel more beloved and more generous. From that new place, you may be comfortable enough to grant your partner whatever you can. You can make individual wish lists and share them with each other if you wish.

A word of caution: Please don't make the requirements too difficult in the beginning. Remember, you're coming from a vulnerable and unsteady place. Your most important goal is to build successive small triumphs. They will give you the confidence to eventually take bigger risks.

Step Six: What Will You Do Differently to Safeguard Your Relationship If It Stumbles in the Future?

In this step, you will create a new set of promises to and for each other. They will become, in essence, relationship vows based upon your new knowledge of each other's wants, vulnerabilities, and capabilities. Because of what you've learned by doing the other exercises, you'll be able to create this commitment based on much clearer probabilities and saner expectations. Knowing and understanding each other from the vantage point of time and experience, you'll be better able to predict and avoid pitfalls and continue to strengthen the bond between you.

Example

Here is a list of promises my clients have made to each other during this step. Again, these are meant only to guide you in forming your own.

- If one of us feels dissatisfied with the relationship, we'll tell each other what we need to make it better, and together we will make a plan for change.

- Each of us will individually continue to grow and bring interesting new experiences to the other.

- We will welcome each other's thoughts and feelings to encourage open sharing without fear of judgment or invalidation.

- We'll make certain that we save prime-time energy for each other no matter what else is going on in our lives.

- Even when we're feeling angry or hurt, we'll try to stay open to each other and not withdraw or withhold our caring.

- We'll always try to resolve our differences by listening deeply to both sides before we create a solution together. If one of us feels abandoned, he or she will reach out to the other and ask for help.

- We'll continually check in with each other to make sure that our goals and dreams are still the same.

Suggestions

These are honorable and effective promises. You won't always remember to keep them, but do strive for continuous improvement. Your pledge to each other must become part of your emotional and spiritual sacred commitment to return to whenever you feel yourselves drifting apart.

Even after you have created these gifts to each other, promise not to punish yourself or your partner if you cannot always follow them exactly as you wish you could. Remember that every day you come closer to becoming the person you want to be, your relationship will improve. Hold on to your promises through the difficult times and have faith that your hard work will pay off.

When you have completed the six steps for each of the stumbles and created your personal promises to each other, remember to revisit those agreements on a regular basis. Keep them visible where both of you can read them every day, and stay open to changing them as you discover new truths.

Reflections

People change. Life delivers unexpected challenges. Blessings and sorrows affect our capacity to live by our commitments. Even when we don't intend it, too much on our plate can take resources away from what we've promised. Integrity can be sacrificed when demands are greater than the resources to meet them.

All great partnerships have two things in common: the people in them live in each other's hearts, and they focus on their commitment to each other when they are in trouble. These are ideals, but every couple can get closer to them.

In the chapters that follow, you will learn how each individual stumble begins, and you'll work through the six steps to understand how to heal them. The more energy you and your partner devote to doing the exercises together, the more you will be able to love each other again.

3

from **fulfillment**
to *disillusionment*

*"You don't seem to care the
way you used to."*

I am always entranced when I watch new lovers anticipate each other's emotions and desires. With little apparent direction, they seem to understand their partner's every thought, facial expression, body movement, and change of mood. To be able to focus so intently on each other, they must temporarily shut out everything else. Producing brain chemicals that make them as connected and adoring as mothers are to new babies, they prioritize their beloved's desires without hesitation or conflict.

New lovers often tell me that they feel as if they've known each other in a past life. How else could they explain their instant rapport and uncanny understanding of each other's unexpressed desires? I hear people say things like this:

"He thinks of what I need before I even realize it."

"She just automatically knows what makes me feel loved."

"I swear, he can read my mind."

"She remembers everything that is important to me. I don't know how she does it."

"He understands me better than I understand myself."

"She just knows how I want to be touched. I don't even have to tell her."

They also feel confident that their passionate, timeless moments will continue forever. The past doesn't matter and the future is secure.

"I love everything about you."

"Promise me you'll never change."

"I want to be with you forever."

"I would do anything to make you happy."

"You're perfect as you are."

As the Relationship Matures

For most of us, those feelings of being deeply known and unconditionally treasured first occurred when we were small children. Protected from the more conditional demands of the outside world, we could express our needs and feel entitled to their fulfillment. As an adult newly in love, we are likely to activate those childhood desires, sharing the words, phrases, and feelings that we remember from that time.

As small children learn that disappointments and disillusionments come with life's challenges, they readjust their expectations and realize that those early experiences must eventually transform into more practical realities. If they have been lucky enough to have been prepared for that transition and still know that they can return for reinforcement, they can survive that process and continue to find success in each new relationship.

Intimate adult partners often go through the same transformation. They enter the delicious and seductive intensity of each new love relationship reliving those early childhood comforts intertwined with the adult capacities of sensual lust and intellectual perspective. As the relationship matures, those original interactions naturally diminish. The partners realize they must refocus their attention on the other priorities in their lives instead of focusing so intensely on each other. They sadly come to understand that they cannot stay forever in the intimate bliss that they have re-created, and may incorrectly believe that their relationship will never be as viable and possibly should end.

If you still love each other and you're still together, but feel that you've lost the wonderful connection that once existed, please do not give up hope. Given the understanding and the tools, you can find that love again. You've merely stumbled and need to get your relationship back on track.

Broken Promises

You were likely sincere and enthusiastic when you made those forever promises to each other when your love was new. Granting each other's wishes, forgiving each other's mistakes, and helping each other feel beloved, you truly felt those commitments would never change.

Like many new lovers, you probably didn't realize you were setting the bar so high. The unmet expectations or mutual disappointments that happen in all relationships may have taken you by surprise. If that has happened, you may have fallen into the trap of trying to convince your partner that his or her expectations are too high or making excuses for your own inability to maintain your original commitments.

Unbridled generosity was a legitimate part of your new love, but it may need to be reevaluated in the light of your current feelings and availability. If you understand that your relationship is changing in a natural way, you can create new expectations in an atmosphere of love and forgiveness.

Is Your Relationship Suffering from Too Many Disappointments?

Long-term committed relationships do not maintain the seemingly infinite resources that you had when your love was new. Other priorities naturally emerge and you may allow life's challenges to draw your attention away from each other. Sometimes it will feel that there just isn't enough love, time, or energy to go around. At times, you may have let things slide without realizing they might be building into big problems that would demand your focus over time.

If you and your partner want to regenerate your faith in each other, you must recommit to staying in touch with each other's individual challenges and changing needs. Crises are bound to happen. Emergencies are part of life. When challenges threaten your commitment to each other, your awareness of your partner's conflicts and desires will help you stay supportive. That way, when stumbles do occur, you can right them quickly.

♥ EXERCISE: Quick Check Disillusionment/Resentment Meter

The following set of questions will help you and your partner evaluate whether your cumulative disappointments have resulted in mutual disillusionment. Using the following scoring system, fill in each blank with the point number that corresponds to your answer.

Open and supportive = 1

Okay but would like something in return = 2

Conflicted but willing to negotiate = 3

Pressured into giving in = 4

Resentful and put out = 5

Angry and not wanting to cooperate = 6

1. When my partner asks me for a favor, I most often feel _____ .

2. When my partner interrupts something I am doing, I most often feel _____ .

3. When my partner asks for my unconditional love and support, I most often feel _____ .

4. When my partner asks for something that is difficult for me to give, I most often feel _____ .

5. When my partner promises that he or she will do something I really want, but asks for something in return, I most often feel _____ .

6. If my partner is more available to others than to me, but asks me for my support, I most often feel _____ .

Scoring

If your individual score is 12 or under, your relationship is in good shape but might need some refreshing. If it is between 13 and 18, your disappointments and resentments are building to an unhealthy level. If your score is over 18, your love is in danger and you'll need to begin your healing plan as soon as possible.

♥

The Healing Plan

To heal resentments from too many disappointments and the unavoidable disillusionment that follows, you'll need to help each other learn to trust again. Though your relationship will never be exactly as it was in its innocence, those attributes that brought you together are still there and can be resurrected.

Step One: Go Back to the Beginning of Your Relationship

Of all the stumbles you will explore in this book, the disappointments that come from unmet expectations are often the most distressing. Because you automatically granted each other's desires when your love was new, it is understandable that you may feel hurt or angry when your needs are no longer being met.

Remembering the sweetness of your earlier devotion is the first step. Even though you will not expect that level of indulgence in every situation, you will still want to count on your partner's generosity at times of legitimate need.

♥ EXERCISE: Early Promises

In the following exercise, you will be asked how you felt about each other before you became disillusioned. Remember the sweetness of feeling understood before you even knew what you needed. Recall as well the many ways you so willingly tried to anticipate your partner's desires and granted them before being asked.

Write several of those experiences in your journal and describe how you felt. Then share them with your partner. This process will help you to fully reexperience those memories and to remember as many of the details as you can.

You may feel discouraged if your earlier experiences felt more fulfilling and aren't happening as often anymore. Please believe you will be able to bring them back.

When each of you has written down your memories, write them in the form of narratives and take turns reading aloud to each other. While sharing them, try to bring back the same emotions you originally felt, remembering the past as accurately as you can.

Example

"I remember how much you liked having me read out loud to you. I used to look for things I knew you'd be interested in, like rare books or the poetry you told me you loved. You would listen so attentively, and you seemed so appreciative. It made me feel like the greatest guy in the world."

Example

"I understood that you could sometimes get lost in whatever you were doing and forget to call when you said you would. I didn't want you to feel guilty or that your behavior was a problem for me, so I'd go out of my way to fill my time with things I loved to do. Then I'd tell you about them and how much I appreciated having the time to take care of myself when you weren't around. I could see the relief on your face and it felt wonderful to me. I wanted you to feel okay about who you were without your feeling you had to change for me. There were so many other things that were easy to love."

Example

"I heard you in my heart when you would tell me how important special occasions were to you, even when they were sad. Remember the time I brought you lilacs when your kitten didn't make it after the accident? You'd told me the month before that they were your favorite flower growing up. I still remember your sweet smile and the tears that wet my shirt when I held you. I would have done anything to make you feel better."

Example

"We'd been together about a year and we were in the mountains for a weekend to ski. There was a terrible snowstorm and we were forced to stay in the cabin. I could tell how frightened you were, though you tried to keep me from knowing. Looking for a way to distract you, I found a book by Walt Whitman on a shelf and asked if I could read it to you. You looked surprised and happy. You told me your grandfather used to read to you during snowstorms and it always made you feel safe. I loved making you feel so loved again."

After sharing each example on your own personal list, ask your partner if he or she remembers that same sweet memory, and talk to each other about any feelings that come up. After sharing each one, try to sit for a while in silence to remember that time together.

♥

Suggestions

Though your renewed memories are positive, you may find yourself contrasting them to the present and feeling sad about what seems to be lost. Please try not to focus on that comparison. As you complete the healing steps, your hope for the future will eclipse those disappointments.

You may need to take a break if an anger bubble emerges or if you are overcome with sadness at the loss. Just tell your partner you need a moment to recover. Holding hands will help you stay connected. When you feel disillusioned from past disappointments, try to let those negative feelings go.

Step Two: Evaluate Your Current Relationship

It is natural for your relationship to lose some of its intensity as you move through life together. If your tender recollections of automatic indulgence remind you that they have not been available for a long while, you may be hesitant to trust each other again.

The exercises in this step are purposefully challenging. You may have some uncomfortable feelings as you recall how much more invested you once were in each other. It is crucial that you not share your disappointments in a punitive way or blame one another for what has been lost. Instead, do your best to let your partner know what you miss most about the early parts of your relationship before those disappointments began.

♥ EXERCISE: Sharing Current Disappointments

Most committed partners remember either having resolved their relationship conflicts along the way or having buried them. They wanted to stay in love and to hold on to the things they valued and enjoyed about the relationship. They chose to make those unmet desires less important by focusing on what was positive and letting negative interactions disperse.

Others didn't give up as easily, and did whatever they could to regain that initial state of generous indulgence they had both experienced. They may have buried their cumulative disappointments in the process. As they could no longer keep them from emerging, they began to feel disillusioned, and are left wondering if anything can be done now to change the situation.

However you and your partner have arrived at where you are, you can bring back your confidence in each other. It may take some time and commitment to look at your situation from a different perspective, but it is surely possible.

Write in your journal about several current desires you have, especially those you wish your partner would have fulfilled without your having to ask. Use the following questions to help guide you as you write your narrative:

What was your desire?

Why was it important to you?

Did you let your partner know what you wanted?

If not, what kept you from doing so?

If you did ask, what did you want to happen?

Did your partner's response disappoint you?

What would you have wanted your partner to do instead?

Did his or her response trigger any memories from your past that influenced your feelings?

Did you harbor any resentment after the incident?

Example

"I really need you to spend some time with me each evening before bedtime and show interest in my day. I've asked you so many times, and I've wanted desperately for it to matter to you as much as it does to me. You make an effort for a little while, and then you get totally involved in other things. You tell me that guys are just that way and their partners have to remind them. Still, I can't help but notice that you seem to remember the things that are important to you.

"My parents both worked nights, and I put myself and my brother to bed. No one ever asked how I was or if I needed anything. I could believe that you love me if I felt that I was important to you in some meaningful way. When you consistently forget, I can only feel like I did then—like no one really cares about who I am. I cry myself to sleep sometimes. I guess I've been really holding on to this hurt."

Example

"You talk all the time about trust and constantly tell me that you're worried about me and other women. I've told you a million times that I'm not the kind of guy who would ever hurt you by being unfaithful. I need more affection, and I've told you how important affection and lovemaking are to me, but you always have an excuse. I've tried every way to make you happy, hoping you would want more closeness as a result. You acknowledge the caring things I do, but they don't seem to make a difference. Just the opposite happens. You come up with a new set of conditions I'm supposed to master for your actions to change.

"I also hate that I'm always the one who brings it up. If you could only see how much I'm suffering inside, why wouldn't you notice and want to make this problem a high priority? If you even just talked to me about it on a regular basis and we could try new things together, I'd feel like I mattered to you again. You keep making promises that you'll be more sexually available, but it never happens. I'm tired of feeling unimportant. Maybe I'm just not desirable. If that's true, why don't you just tell me? I act like this is less important than it is, but I'm really angry about this situation."

After sharing each of your own examples, ask your partner for his or her responses. As the reader or listener, do not erase or invalidate your partner's experience. Just listen carefully and try to understand. Also, don't defend your own experiences if you feel your partner doesn't understand. Each of you should try to hear what the other is saying without challenge or invalidation.

♥

♥ EXERCISE: Contrasting Now with Then

For each example on your request/disappointment lists, ask each other how you would have responded differently to the same request when your love was new. In a simple narrative, tell your partner about each experience.

He or she may feel guilty or defensive when you share your disappointments and eventual disillusionment. Assure your partner that you don't want to hurt him or her. This exercise is not meant to create animosity or resentment, just to contrast where you've been with where you are now.

Example

"I don't want to hurt you by saying this, but I've agreed to be honest, so I need to take that chance. I still love you, honey, but I am pretty disappointed in a lot of ways.

"When we were first in love, I used to think you were psychic. I felt like you lived in my heart and always knew what I wanted before I even did. Even more than that, you seemed to want to please me even when it meant going out of your way to do it. You never seemed resentful.

"Lately, I feel like you just plug me into your own script and expect me to be whatever you want. I still try to let you know what's really important to me, but you seem to have taken me off your radar.

"Sometimes it even feels purposeful, like you need to get back at me for something, or you just don't care that much any more. When I try to let you know how I feel, you always say you're sorry, but nothing seems to change. I miss the partner who always knew what I wanted before I did and couldn't wait to surprise me. I realize that it would be unrealistic to expect you to read my mind, but it felt so amazing when you used to try. Even if things are different now, just knowing that you care would give me hope again."

♥

Suggestions

It is natural to feel current disappointments more deeply when you contrast them to an earlier, more satisfying time. If you feel saddened or disillusioned, revisit the exercise in Step One to remember the tender feelings you once had for each other. Those memories will help you stay connected through these next exercises.

Step Three: When Did You Begin to Drift?

Many times couples are confused as to how and when they began drifting apart. Because each of you may experience crucial incidents differently, and may not have the same resilience for resolving them, it is important that you recall those memories and share why and how they were important at the time. Learning when and why those chasms occurred can help you prevent them in the future.

Perhaps unpredicted stressors demanded your attention and redirected your energy. You may actually have planned to recommit to each other when those pressures abated, but you became preoccupied with other pressing issues. Or you might have had separate opportunities for growth that took energy away from your relationship, and then you never made each other a priority again in the same way.

It is crucially important that both of you remember when that wondrously indulgent love first began to wane. Perhaps it was different for each of you. You needn't have similar reasons for being less motivated or have equally intense responses. It doesn't matter. This is not the time for blame, punishment, or keeping score. You're here to just teach each other what events and responses took you from each other.

♥ EXERCISE: When I Began Feeling Less Motivated to Anticipate Your Desires

Pick three examples of situations when you didn't want to fulfill your partner's desires. Talk about what you knew he or she wanted and what you did instead. Recall what was going on inside of you and why you chose that time to withhold instead of granting that desire.

Example

"I remember the night of our third anniversary and how much I wanted you to make it special for me. We'd been a little estranged for awhile, and I was hoping you'd want to do something to bring us closer. I'd spent the afternoon cooking your favorite dinner and sent the baby to your mom's for the night. I wanted it to be just you and me, like when we fell in love.

"I must have told you a hundred times how important it was that you made it home from work on time that night. I even called your boss and got him to agree to let you out early. I bought new lingerie and had it on under that funny long coat you wore in college so long ago. I wanted to make you simultaneously laugh and desire me.

"It was eleven o'clock and you still weren't home. I thought of calling the police, half hoping you were in jail or something else legitimate. Climbing into your side of the bed, I pretended you were near me and cried myself to sleep, and something died inside. You woke me up at midnight, filled with excuses and remorse, but it didn't matter. You had promised you'd always be there for me if I needed you, but I stopped believing it that night. I remember promising myself that I wouldn't do anything special for you anymore. It just felt too one-sided."

Example

"I'd been asking you for years if we could just spend one Christmas alone together without obligations to family members. Maybe in some romantic spot where we could make time stand still the way we used to.

"You'd pay lip service each year in January and promise me that next Christmas would be our time away. You even said you wanted the same. Then, as the holidays approached, you'd begin your pitch: Your mother's sadness. Your dad's illness that might make this the last Christmas with him. Your sister's drug addiction and threatened suicides. There was always an excuse. I didn't stand a chance.

"I remember feeling like a fool, more so than ever before. I didn't want to remember any more what was important to you, or to be expected to remember what made you feel special. I'd always be there if you asked, but no more guessing and surprising you. I can't keep doing this without feeling your love in return."

When you recall these potentially hurtful and often buried memories, please ask your partner to simply listen compassionately and not argue. Your stories may be difficult for you to share and equally hard for your partner to hear.

By the time you have each shared at least three examples, you may be able to discern a thread of similarity among them. That similar core may help you understand why you gave up wanting to love as you did before. How many times have you felt the same feelings of exclusion, lack of importance, or devaluation when your partner disappointed you?

Try to help each other find whatever similarities exist in both of your descriptions of the same memory. All couples have repeated patterns that, once identified, can be more easily healed.

♥

Step Four: What Got in the Way of Healing Your Stumble at the Time?

Committed couples often take each other for granted. Without even realizing it, they can become preoccupied with other choices and forget the promises they've made. They may not notice how much they are neglecting each other, or how their security and trust will be damaged if they don't resolve their situation.

Reversing your roles in Step Three above will help you look at your own behavior when you have disappointed your partner. It is often more comfortable to believe that the fault is mostly with your partner, but you will limit your learning process if you do.

Self-accountability will give you the understanding to make a real difference and will help your partner feel better about owning his or her own participation when you reverse the roles.

♥ EXERCISE: What Could I Have Done to Right the Situation When It Occurred?

Write in your journal about several times in the past when your partner wanted something important from you and you either did not recognize it, or didn't want to grant that desire. Your partner may have even told you how much that hurt, or asked you to reconsider, but you chose not to.

Begin your narrative with what the request was, what you chose to do instead, and why you made that decision. Add how you believe your partner may have felt and what happened between the two of you as a result.

When you share those realizations with your partner, request that he or she not comment. It is too easy to jump on the bandwagon when someone is vulnerable, and you mustn't attack each other when you are open. That would only strengthen your defenses and interfere with your willingness to look at your own responsibility in the future.

Example

"I knew you loved your religion and practiced it in every way you could. When we were first together, you talked all about it and I was totally willing to learn whatever you wanted to share. I loved how you always helped people. We talked many times about my joining you in prayer, and I always said I would some day. It didn't much matter to me, but I knew it was important to you.

"When your brother was diagnosed with his life-threatening illness, you began going to church every day to ask for God's help. You wanted me to go with you, but I never seemed to make it. I knew you were disappointed, but I didn't change my actions. I guess I just wasn't willing to make it that important or give it that much credibility.

"When he died, you didn't want me at his funeral. You told me that I'd never understand because I didn't believe in God's will. Hell, I think I even responded by mocking any God who would let that happen. I know now how much it hurt you. We didn't get close again for months. I just didn't get it, and maybe I resented always coming second to your faith.

"Now I do go to church with you from time to time. I know you appreciate it and in many ways seem to have let go of the past. But I know somewhere inside, you've never forgiven me. I wish I'd understood better. I would never have hurt you that deeply if I'd known."

Example

"I know how you love to eat healthy foods and work out all the time. When we were first together, I promised you I'd commit to that same lifestyle because it was so important to you. I was really good at the beginning, but after a while I kept putting other things first. You tried really hard to get me to keep my promise, but I guess it just wasn't that important to me, and I made decisions to do the things I wanted instead.

"You started spending a lot of time away from me and making comments about other women who were in great shape. We fought about it all the time. Now I can see that I just attacked you for not accepting me the way I am, rather than admit that I'd let you down. I did sell you a bum deal and it's my responsibility to fix it."

Please use the following set of descriptive behaviors to strengthen your commitment to each other. They may be hard to own and can activate your defenses. Because you are in this together, you can support each other's willingness to be open and accountable. The more willing you are to do this exercise together, the closer you will be when you are finished.

- You made a promise to fulfill a desire that you would have done willingly at the beginning of your relationship, but at some point you no longer felt the need to follow through.

- You broke that promise and disappointed your partner.

- You made excuses for why you didn't come through.

- A rift occurred between you that lay unresolved.

- You didn't do what you could have to heal the separation at the time.

- You now want to make amends by taking responsibility for your past decisions.

- You're willing to change that behavior in the future.

When you and your partner each finish this exercise, you will hopefully feel encouraged in a new way. Self-accountability is the first step in the promise that things can change.

♥

Step Five: What Do You Need from Each Other to Trust Again?

The exercise in this next step will take you further into your vulnerability and will test how committed you are to regenerating your love. When you tell each other about what you need to open your hearts again, your partner might not be able to give it to you. The chance that he or she may is always worth fighting for.

The most important thing you can each do now is to whole-heartedly take that chance again. Having visited memories of how much you once loved each other and how you want that love again, you can see the value in taking those risks.

When you do the following exercise, face each other, speak slowly, and maintain some kind of physical contact, even if it is one finger touching. Do not look away from one another. Looking into each other's eyes during vulnerable times is the beginning of true intimacy. Considering all of the negatives you have been willing to reveal, you have little to lose and everything to gain.

♥ EXERCISE: What I Need to Trust You Again

Write in your journal five things you would love for your partner to give you. They can be physical, emotional, sexual, or spiritual requests. Add enough details that your desire is easy to understand and possible to grant.

Your partner may not want to, or be able to, give you exactly what you would like, but he or she will at least know what a "10" is. You're not looking to be an indulged child or a pampered adult. Your partner's goal is to master your most delicious desires that he or she feels confident to give.

Make your initial requests simple, to help your partner build confidence and motivation. There will be many more opportunities to try again later with more complicated and emotionally risky requests.

After each request, ask for your partner's honest response. If he or she cannot give you exactly what you want, accept what is offered and appreciate the effort for now. Because you have been practicing withholding from each other, respond with as much enthusiasm as you honestly can. This is a process, not a conclusion, and will hopefully be part of your partnership from now on.

Example

"This request is more general, and I hope I can communicate what I need from you without specifics right now. I have felt disillusioned because I have been disappointed so many times. It's about your response when I want to share something that is important to me but not necessarily to you. When I do, you look uncomfortable at best and disinterested and bored at the worst. I end up feeling embarrassed and really unloved.

"I guess I want you to take me seriously when I share special experiences in my life, even if they aren't really interesting to you. I'd feel so beloved if you'd look at me when I'm talking and try to stretch a little into my world. I want to feel closer to you, and I can't do that if I always live in yours. I know you don't like it when I sometimes go into too much detail, but I think I would be less wordy if you seemed genuinely interested."

Example

"Sometimes I need to complain about something you did that hurt me. I'm not trying to punish you or make you feel guilty, but I don't want to have to worry about your feelings when I need you to know how I feel. I want you to let me vent and not argue or get defensive or tell me how it's my fault. Just support me even if you don't agree or if you have a different idea about what happened."

Example

"I need you to let me in on your plans before you make decisions that affect us both. It's like you don't want my input, so you make things happen before I can vote. It's a no-win situation; I'll be a jerk if I don't go along, or a fool if I keep accepting your control issues. I'm not promising that I won't try to stop things if I don't like them, but at least I'd feel that I matter. It would make a hell of a difference in the way I participate. I'm sorry I'm so angry, but I've been holding this in for a long time. I really want to trust you the way I used to."

♥

Suggestions

Your personal statements to each other should be sacred to both of you. They come from a new place of vulnerability, and they need to be heard with respect and compassion. Whether you can open your hearts to give in the same intuitive and generous way you once did will depend on the honesty and love with which you value those requests.

Step Six: What Will You Do Differently to Prevent Future Disappointments?

Your future plans depend on what both of you want from the relationship and from each other. You both have your own personal challenges and stressors, and they must be met with the resources you have available. Yet, within those assets and restrictions, you must create a mutual plan that will give you both hope again.

The new commitment you create together must be a living entity, subject to revision and reexamination as you learn more about each other's wants and sorrows as time passes. At any one moment, it is the sacred promise you hold together; the basis for your love to grow beyond the disappointment stumbles you have created and the disillusion that has followed them.

To ensure that you have the best chance, promise each other that you will keep the following guidelines in your hearts at all times:

- Inform your partner of what you have to offer, and take responsibility for your limitations when you can't do more.

- Be willing to maintain a consistent commitment to keep your promises and not blame your partner if you are unable to follow through.

- Stay willing to share the deepest parts of yourself as an ongoing process.

- Always keep your partner aware of your desires so that you can help him or her not miss important cues.

- Live in each other's hearts and thoughts. Stay current so that you can avoid unexpected disappointments.

- Support each other's little stumbles and help each other get back up and recommit.

- Stay committed to regeneration.

Example

"I'm thinking of all the well-intentioned promises I've made to you over the years, and I'm embarrassed about my batting average. I tend to agree to things without thinking them through, and when I forget that I've committed to conflicting priorities, sometimes I can't deliver. I'm going to do my best to predict my true capabilities and either tell you I can't do what you've asked or come through for you.

I won't make excuses anymore or try to minimize your past disappointments.

"I want you to know who I really am, and I hope you will still love me when you do. I want to think about what is in your heart and make sure you feel heard and supported by me, especially when I can't help you. Most importantly, please forgive me if I slip up occasionally. I could not bear to lose you, and I'll give this everything I've got."

Each week, use these guidelines to create simple promises to grant your partner the special behavior he or she has asked of you. Express them from your heart and tell your partner exactly what part of his or her desire you can or cannot fulfill. Then keep that promise.

Check in frequently with your partner to make certain you are doing what he or she wanted and what you have promised. Ask for support and encouragement. Put each week's promise creed some-where both of you can see it every day. Repeat this exercise until the capacity to recognize your partner's needs becomes a way of life for both of you.

Reflections

Life's transitions change people, but there is no intimate relationship that can bear the continuous breaking of commitments and prom-ises. Expectations that become continuous disappointments make partners lose trust in love and leave disillusionment in their wake.

No one person can be everything to another, but partners should ideally be clear about what they can and cannot offer. The four most crucial commitments are:

- Be honest about what you are able to give.

- Let your partner know what you need in return.

- Only promise what you know you can deliver.

- Whenever possible, deliver more than you promised.

These sacred commitments are major players if couples genuinely want to meet each other's expectations. Knowing what the parameters are, loving couples can more easily forgive when unexpected life events interfere and still look forward to trusting that agreed-upon expectations will become joyful realities.

4

from **excitement**
to *boredom*

"What happened to our spark?"

I ask each new couple two important questions: what attracted you
to each other when you first met, and why did you decide to commit
to a relationship?

Though lasting love can sometimes develop after people have
known each other for some time, most tell me they knew they had
found the right person within hours of their first meeting. They
liked the energy between them. They were physically attracted. Time
stood still. Lust was aroused. But there was more. It felt magnetic,
like two halves of something that hadn't felt whole until then.

"I couldn't get enough of her. The evening ended too
soon."

"Ten minutes into our date, I felt more excited about him
than anyone I'd met in years."

"I couldn't stop looking at him. It was almost embarrassing."

"Time disappeared when I was with her. I can't remember the last time I was so intrigued."

"I can't really tell you why. Yes, he was handsome, but it was more than that. Every cell in my body was alive when I left him."

"She was adorable, of course. But it was the way she was so open and—I don't know—fascinating. I felt excited just to be with her."

The similar element in all these responses is a sense of surprised awakening. These people felt positively changed in a delicious way. They didn't need to know why. They just knew it felt wonderful, and they wanted more.

The Common Quest

People searching for a new relationship use every resource they have to find and capture the most desirable person they can. When a potential partner responds positively, an upward spiral begins and the new lovers continue to validate each other with each subsequent encounter.

As they spend more time together, they uncover layers of each other's past and their current desires. Their sexual, intellectual, philosophical, emotional, cultural, and familial explorations continue to expand and deepen. If those discoveries bring more intrigue and excitement, the relationship continues with an exhilarating intensity and the couple falls more deeply in love.

Security Becomes More Important

As new lovers spend more time together, the intensity of their initial emotional and sexual energy quiets and they are not likely to make as many new discoveries about one another. The exquisite anticipation of continuous discovery transforms into the greater desire for the comfort of familiarity and security. They must now incorporate the other priorities they've neglected into their new relationship and face the realities of their life as a permanent couple.

As they focus on blending two lives into one, the partners may forget to maintain the exciting differences and new discoveries that attracted them to each other when they were newly in love. Content to settle for the sweetness of predictability, they may not realize that too much security can easily tempt them into passivity.

In time, the partners may begin to feel restless. Seduced by the comfort of knowing each other too well, they may drift into laziness, no longer putting forth the energy that regenerated and recharged the relationship in its early days.

Is Your Relationship Suffering from Diminished Excitement?

*   Have you noticed that you are less interested when your partner shares his or her experiences with you?

*   Do you find that you are not as motivated to share special moments with your partner?

*   Do you feel bored when your partner is sharing the same stories you've heard before, even if it's with someone you've both just met?

*   Are you losing interest in your partner because he or she is too predictable?

*   Does your partner seem unresponsive when you attempt to get him or her interested in new directions?

*   Do you find yourself more apathetic than alive in your relationship?

If you and your partner realize that you are much less excited by each other than you once were, you may have tipped the balance in the direction of too much security and not enough excitement. Though you still care deeply for one another and have no desire to leave the relationship, you may have lost the spark that kept you wanting more. Perhaps you have sadly accepted what you thought was the inevitable price of a long-term partnership but still yearn for what once was.

Or, more hopefully, you have not given up. At moments you still look at each other across a room and feel remnants of that wonderful thrill you once were guaranteed. You know there must be a way to find that again, but you don't know quite what to do.

♥ EXERCISE: Quick Check Relationship Excitement Meter

The following set of statements will help you and your partner evaluate the current level of excitement in your relationship. Using the scoring system below, fill in the blanks with the corresponding point number.

As you write in your journal, add any pertinent thoughts that can identify how you feel toward your partner at this time.

Excited and eager to connect again = 1

Somewhat excited but don't sustain interest = 2

Only excited if there is reciprocal interest = 3

Bored but somewhat available = 4

Not very interested or excited = 5

Not at all interested = 6

1. When my partner asks me to spend time with him or her, I am often _____ .

2. If my partner wants to share something with me, I am often _____ .

3. If my partner has been gone a while and returns home, I am often _____ .

4. When I'm out doing something social with my partner, I am often _____.

5. When my partner wants me to be intimate, I am often _____.

6. If my partner shows enthusiasm about something, I am often _____.

7. If I want to share something I'm excited about, my partner is often _____.

8. When I show interest in something my partner is doing, he or she is often _____.

9. If I tell my partner that I want to do something new together, he or she is often _____.

10. If I share something that happened during my day, my partner is often _____.

Scoring

If your individual score is 20 or less, your relationship still holds a significant amount of excitement and challenge. If it is between 21 and 40, your lack of excitement and the danger it heralds may be building to an unhealthy level. If your score is over 40, your interest in each other is in jeopardy and you'll need to begin your healing plan as soon as possible.

♥

The Healing Plan

The six steps of your healing plan will help you to regenerate excitement in your relationship. Going through the exercises, you will:

• Reexperience your original excitement.

• Contrast those early feelings with what you are feeling now.

• Remember when and why the excitement began to diminish.

- Re-create those sparks in the present.

- Be able to create those exciting feelings again.

As you do the exercises, you may feel vulnerable, embarrassed, or sad when you and your partner realize how far you have drifted. Please don't. You were highly motivated when you first met, and that unbridled enthusiasm naturally generated excitement. Novel experiences and intriguing challenges wane over time if no new transformations emerge.

Step One: Go Back to the Beginning of Your Relationship

When you were focusing all of your energy on each other in the early days, you probably didn't worry about whether those physical and emotional bonfires would continue to burn as brightly in the future. Although it can be discouraging to realize that the excitement between you has diminished, don't invalidate your memories. Those memories are real and the feelings that accompanied them were authentic. Though those exquisite, timeless moments may now happen less frequently, you are still those same people somewhere inside. Now is the time to find them again.

♥ EXERCISE: What Did You Find Exciting About Your Partner When Your Love Was New?

In your journal, write down any of your partner's emotional, physical, sexual, spiritual, or intellectual behaviors or qualities that intrigued you in the beginning of your relationship. Concentrate on those that were particularly poignant and bring back tender memories.

When you have these elements firmly in mind, write a love letter to your partner as if you were feeling that initial attraction again. In your letter, describe those behaviors and characteristics and how they made you feel at the time. If you have a picture of your partner that was taken at that time, place it in front of you when you are writing to help you remember.

As you are going through this exercise, please do not talk about things that naturally alter with time. Your partner cannot help that he has less hair, or that her breasts are not as firm as they once were. This exercise will work better if you concentrate on the more important and lasting positive dimensions of a relationship, like great personality characteristics and desirable values.

Example

Characteristics:

- You were so hilarious. You made me laugh in a way I never had before.

- I loved the way you caressed my hair when I'd put my head in your lap.

- I remember when you tried to wash my kitten after she threw up. You used an entire box of bandages on the scratches she gave you.

- It was those beautiful, long legs. The first time I saw you in shorts, I couldn't take my eyes off you.

- You introduced me to fantasy science fiction and shared your visions of being one of those heroes.

- You had this great way of avoiding eye contact when you had a surprise for me.

- I loved when you were passionate about your God.

Example

"Dearest one,
"I'm looking at you now and remembering when we first met.
Those dancing eyes and the mischief behind them always

got me. I remember when your mom died and your tears when we went to your church to pray for her. No matter what was happening in your life, sad or joyous, you always were passionate about it. Your way of looking at life made me feel more alive than I'd ever felt before. I could listen to your childhood stories or about a fight with your boss. It didn't matter. The way you would make them come to life was amazing. You made everything into a movie I didn't want to miss."

Example

"Sweetheart,

"I remember studying day and night in graduate school. I was irritable and agitated most of the time. The day you came into my life, the sun came out. You'd walk in the door, filled with some silly idea that we needed to go immediately and feed the frogs at the park because they would starve to death that afternoon if we didn't. You gave me your famous quizzical look, as if I'd be a fool to argue with something so obvious. The studying always got done later, but I wasn't angry anymore with you at my side.

"I learned to hop and skip from you. Somehow I missed that lesson in nursery school. You could really make me laugh, whether we were stoned or sober. I never felt bored, not even for a moment. I felt like I finally understood why people fall in love."

♥

Suggestions

Remembering these early experiences can be poignant, especially if you haven't let yourself feel those kinds of feelings in a long time. Uncovering once-tender feelings can hurt if they are less frequent now. Remember, you are reexperiencing ways of being that are hopefully not gone, only dormant. Let yourself feel those moments again, even if they make you sad. Your goal is to want them again.

Step Two: Evaluate Your Current Relationship

This may be the most difficult of your healing steps. In sharing long-withheld feelings and thoughts, you may be opening yourself to disappointing feelings when you contrast the past with the present. You may feel reluctant to talk too openly about your disappointments and sorrows, concerned that they could expose the compromises you've made to stay together.

It is natural to feel that way, but unexpressed feelings of discontent do much more damage to a relationship in the long run. Once you are able to share your deepest sorrows with each other and still feel beloved, you will open the door to a new kind of intimacy. Throughout these exercises you will be reminded to pay attention to the positive interactions that still exist. Support each other in this process. It will help give you the confidence you need to push through the harder moments.

Boredom: The Enemy of Sustained Intimacy

The diminished energy that accompanies a too-predictable encounter is the most frequent symptom of lessened excitement in a relationship. It is often not identified for what it is, because it usually develops slowly and may be eclipsed by other attachments. Partners who have been lured by the familiarity of comfort and predictability often do not realize that they have stopped seeking the novelty that keeps boredom at bay.

Apathy and irritability are the two major symptoms of boredom. Together they create an emotional atmosphere of dispassionate tension. Partners who are bored with each other feel disconnected and reactive at the same time.

Apathy is manifested as a lack of passion, emotion, or excitement. When the partners in a relationship feel that deadness, they either avoid each other or interact with impatience and minimal interest. Over time, they usually stop trying to connect, expecting rejection or a lack of response.

People who are bored are unable to bear frustration. They often respond to requests for connection with irritation because they feel restless and entrapped. What might have once been a constant discovery of unknown treasures has now become a monotonous parade of predictable same-olds.

If you are feeling apathetic about your relationship, your desire to escape may be in competition with your desire to stay. You may be feeling resentment, martyrdom, and the desire to blame your partner, picking on him or her for little things. You might even create dysfunctional interactions as a poor substitute for the excitement you are missing.

In the following exercises, try to be accountable for your own behavior. Though it may be easier to blame your partner for your dissatisfactions, you'll have more luck in growing past your limitations if you are in touch with your own contributions.

♥ EXERCISE: Apathetic Responses

In your journal, describe at least two recurring situations when you asked your partner to share an experience and he or she responded apathetically. Include background information, emotions, and any pertinent details.

Next, reverse the roles, and similarly describe at least two different situations when you were the one who responded apathetically to your partner's attempt to connect.

Your goal in both examples is to contrast how you responded when your love was new with how you would respond in the present.

When you are satisfied with your examples, write a narrative in your journal that you will share with your partner. Remember, these individual examples needn't have the same importance to both of you. Listen with respect, even if you don't see things the same way.

Example

"One of my favorite things about our relationship used to be when we would take a shower together before going to bed. The warm water and being naked with you felt incredibly sensual and sweet. You seemed to want it as much as I did.

Now when I ask, you talk about how tired you are, or you hardly respond at all. I know I should just let go, but it still hurts every time."

"I know I should care more when you complain about your boss, but frankly, I'm kind of bored with the whole thing. There was a time when I really cared about what happened and wanted to be part of the solution. I finally realized that you never listened to my advice or changed your behavior, so why should I care anymore?"

♥

♥ EXERCISE: Irritated Responses

Now do the same with two typical interactions where you respond with impatience or irritation. Then, as above, reverse the roles and complete the rest of the exercise. Remember to include as many details as you can.

Example

"I sometimes need a few minutes of your time to reassure me that you're still interested in what's going on with me. Even when I wait until you seem more available, you generally snap at me as if I'm bothering you. When I ask what's going on, you patronize me with some stupid excuse about needing time alone or being overloaded. Come on, so much of the time?

"Then, when you realize I'm obviously hurt by your lack of caring, you try to listen, but you're clearly feeling impatient, as if you want me to get it over with quickly. If you're so bored with me, can you just be honest? This really feels terrible.

"You used to be so patient with me, even when I was so incompetent in getting my ideas across. It's painful to know now that you are so uninterested."

Example

"I get pissed when you constantly interrupt me with irrelevant questions when I'm doing something important. I react as if you wait for the moment when it will really irritate me. I'm usually more patient with other people, but I seem to expect more from you. I wish I were more tolerant.

"I think I'm oversensitive because I bury my feelings when I'm hurt and it comes out in unfair sniping."

♥

Suggestions

Your examples may be uncomfortable for your partner to hear, even if he or she knows they do happen. Show compassion both in sharing your honest feelings and in responding to your partner's responses. If your relationship has become boring, you are both responsible. Judgment of each other will set you back. You're searching to understand how you got this way so you can regain your original vitality.

Step Three: When Did You Begin to Drift?

Partners who once found so much excitement together did not lose that excitement overnight. New love manufactures energy as a by-product of discovery and novelty. That in turn gives new partners abundant motivation to excite and to please. It is a delicious upward spiral.

Committed partners usually want the best for each other, but can easily slip in their devotion when they direct their resources away from their primary relationship. They may have made security so important that the passion they once felt for each other has been sacrificed. Basking in that comfort, many couples forget the need to maintain the excitement that brought them together. Ask yourself to remember when you stopped trying to create those moments of aliveness.

♥ EXERCISE: The First Realization

Whether the excitement in your relationship diminished slowly or quickly, you can recall moments when you realized things had changed. You may have avoided paying attention to them because you hoped they would go away. For those reasons, they may be hard to remember, but doing so is important to healing this stumble.

Recall the first time you were clearly aware of feeling apathetic or irritable in an interaction with your partner. Pick an example where you would have had more interest and patience in a similar situation in the past.

In your journal, write down as many details as you can, such as:

- What was the situation?

- Where were you?

- Did anything unusual precede the interaction?

- Did you talk to your partner at the time about your feelings?

- If so, how did your partner respond?

- Whether you communicated or not, how did you feel?

- How important was the experience for you?

Once you have written the details as best as you can remember, use them to write a short narrative to read to your partner.

Example

"I do remember the moment I realized you didn't care about my feelings like you once did. I didn't make it a big deal at the time, because I was afraid you'd be angry with me.

"You were out at a hockey game with your good friends and promised you'd be home early because we were going skiing together the next morning. You came home at 3:00 a.m., wasted, and hadn't responded to any of my calls as the time grew later.

"When you came in, I asked you where you'd been and why you hadn't called me. You snapped at me and told me I sounded like your mother and you didn't need parenting anymore. You said it was none of my business what you did with your friends and I was overreacting and needed to get off your back.

"It was the first time you'd ever talked to me like that. I felt my heart drop. You were obviously more excited by what you were doing than by being with me. I pulled in and didn't respond. Something broke inside, and I don't think I ever went back to feeling the way I did before."

Example

"After we moved into the new house, there was a never-ending list of things that 'had to be done.' At first it was okay, watching things improve and seeing the look of gratitude and happiness on your face when they did. Eventually, I got sick of having you plan my existence, not allowing me any guilt-free time for myself. I remember telling you repeatedly that I needed to look forward to something fun once in a while, that there were too many obligations in my life. You couldn't hear me, or didn't want to.

"I found a hundred legitimate ways to get out from under those demands so I didn't have to feel like a shirker or spend all my time working on the house. I was bored and restless, and I'm sure you felt it. We did get the house done eventually, but I never really got excited about creating things together again."

♥

Suggestions

When you talk with your partner about being bored, be careful to describe the specific situation you are talking about. If you allow yourselves to start dredging up every other complaint, you will overload your partner with too much criticism. As a result, he or she will become defensive and have a hard time hearing the importance of your message.

Recall the rules for caring and effective communication:

1. Use simple sentences.

2. Express your feelings without accusations.

3. Listen from your heart.

4. Don't interrupt.

5. Stay open and nondefensive.

6. Take a break if either of you feels too distressed.

7. Check in often with your partner to make sure you're on the same page.

8. Stay kind.

These simple guidelines will help you if your emotions begin to interfere with your goals. You're in this process together, gathering crucial information to help you regain the excitement you've lost.

Step Four: What Stopped You from Keeping Your Excitement Alive?

The excitement of new love will naturally diminish somewhat as couples intertwine their dreams, goals, resources, and baggage. Committed partners should not expect that the moment-to-moment thrill of the initial passion will be ever-present, but they should feel confident that they can bring it back.

You must also take responsibility for why you may be feeling apathetic or bored for reasons that are outside of your relationship. Too much dependency on your partner can be the result of your own self-boredom. You could try bringing something novel to the table yourself, or responding in a fresh way to your partner's efforts to start the upward spiral you desire.

The following exercise will help you remember how you may have put up barriers when your partner reached out to you for excitement. Stay with your own contribution to the situation, and do not focus on your partner's behavior.

♥ EXERCISE: Excitement Barriers

Ask yourself to recall situations when your partner wanted a more exciting interaction with you, and you rejected the offer. Try to remember in detail what was going on at the time and why you were not interested in your partner's request.

Remember that self-accountability does not need to be self-recrimination. It is simply the willingness to look clearly at what you may have done to contribute to your present situation. This may not be easy to do. It is typical to point fingers when you are unhappy. However, in order for you to regain what you have lost, both you and your partner must agree to look at your own accountability when you have turned each other away.

When you share your most embarrassing moments with your partner, he or she should listen without judgment and try not to defend by reversing the blame. Confessions made from the heart are good material for eventual forgiveness.

In your journal, write about at least two situations where you rejected your partner's offer to revitalize your relationship. Recall as much of the situation as you can, including how you were feeling at the time, why you chose to not accept the invitation, and how you are feeling now about your decision. When you have created your narrative, read it aloud and ask for support and understanding.

Example

"I'm embarrassed to share this with you because I think I unfairly blamed you when it happened. I should have told you at the time and tried to work it out, but I'd been angry at you for neglecting me and I wanted to make you the one who was wrong.

"We were at that little bed-and-breakfast place where we always went to reconnect. Part of me wanted to be there, but I was conflicted. I'd been ripped up inside, wanting you to succeed at your new job, but wanting to be number one in your life at the same time. I felt really stupid, like if I, as a guy, were in your position, I'd expect you to understand. I knew it was completely wrong to feel that way, but my ego got in the way.

"You'd put in a lot of time and energy to make that weekend perfect, and you were probably trying to make up to me for the times you'd been away. I think I knew that, but I pretended it didn't matter. I could have really helped make our time together exciting, but I was punishing you.

"You put on that really sexy lingerie and served me the wine you know I love. I wasn't having any of it. I think I watched two football games in a row, and then told you I was too tired to have sex that night. I saw the disappointment in your eyes, but I didn't care.

"You never even got angry. You just cuddled up against me and told me that whatever I wanted was okay. I think I turned self-righteousness into the right to reject you because of how you'd neglected me, and I've probably done that ever since. I can't believe you've been so incredibly supportive throughout this, and I wish I had acted differently. I feel like a real jerk. Can you forgive me?"

♥

Suggestions

This is the time for your partner to stay openhearted even though he or she may feel angry or want to retaliate. It's embarrassing and difficult for anyone to admit they've been at fault, particularly when it's an important situation. The more both of you can feel received and supported when you share your narratives, the more open you will continue to be. This is an exercise that gets easier and more effective with repetition.

Step Five: What Do You Need from Each Other to Bring Excitement Back into Your Relationship?

Hopefully, you are now in touch with the excitement you once felt for each other and how much of it you may have lost. Old resentments and unhealed wounds can threaten when you begin the process of resolution. Try to keep them from sabotaging your healing as you build hope for reconnection.

Sometimes reactivating positive behaviors from the past can actually regenerate excitement. You may feel wonderfully nostalgic as you remember them together. Those memories are not enough in and of themselves to heal the present and change the future, but they will give you a template of what is possible.

Self-Transformation as an Antidote

After an extended period of time together, two people who have not evolved or transformed will eventually lack passion for each other. It is relatively easy to master another person's repertoire given many interactions over a long period of time. When partners are able to easily predict each other's ideas, behaviors, attitudes, and philosophies, they cease to be actively attentive.

Though all intimate partners derive some comfort from familiarity, there must be continued challenge and discovery for relationships to stay alive. Renewed excitement for each other will come as you recommit to bring back the novelty, challenge, and love of newness you once took so much for granted.

If you want to maintain spontaneous delight in each other's company, you must commit to continually searching for your own personal transformation, growing from your experiences, and deepening your involvement in life and your relationship. If you have a mutual quest to enrich your own life and your partner's, your chances of staying excited about your relationship will be significantly greater.

♥

♥ EXERCISE: Please Do's and Please Don'ts List

The goal of this exercise is to give your partner an exact and direct list of those behaviors that are likely to regenerate excitement and interest in you and those that will produce the opposite effect.

Remember, these requests are not obligations to fulfill, but simply accurate guides for you to better understand each other's desires. If you're going to get a grade on what you do for each other, it's always nice to know which behaviors would earn an "A."

To help your partner clarify what response he or she can expect, put a number from one to ten after each one of your requests, corresponding to the level of importance you give to that request. Higher numbers equal greater importance. That will help your partner understand your reactions when you share your lists with each other.

As you write these in your journal, please be as honest as you can. If you're like many couples, you've never laid out the excitement/satisfaction desires alongside the boring/dissatisfaction dislikes for comparison.

The more you're willing to risk here, the better your chance of getting some of what you're looking for. The examples on the lists below may seem to represent only traditional male or female values. However, I have had both genders describe themselves in all of them.

Example

List One: Excitement Do's

- I would be excited if you would plan an evening for us and not tell me what we're going to do. 10

- I would be excited if you would read parts of a book out loud with me before we go to bed each night. 7

- I would be excited if you would work out with me and help me stay on track. 9

- I would be excited if you wore sexier underwear. 8

- I would be excited if you could stay up later with me at night sometimes. 6

- I would be excited if you wrote me poetry. 10

- I would be excited if you watched basketball with me and actually enjoyed it. 8

List Two: Boring Don'ts

- I'm bored when you talk on the phone to your friends at night. 10

- I'm bored when you complain about the same things over and over. 10

- I'm bored when we only have sex in the mornings. 8

- I'm bored when you play computer games. 9

- I'm bored when you get animated with other people and ignore me. 9

- I'm bored when you always have one more thing to do when we need to go. 8

- I'm bored when you sleep late in the mornings. 8

In this example, the excitement value in the first list would add up to 58 out of a possible 70 points, and the boring behaviors in the second list would add up to 62 out of 70. Though the scores are relatively close, the direction could be potentially negative.

Create original items to make the exercise work best for your relationship. You can use either list as coming from you or from your partner. What is important is that you share all aspects of this interaction. That process will help to bring your passion back.

♥

Suggestions

These lists should ideally be updated every month of your lives together. You can cross off uncontested items as they become part of your relationship, and add things that you become newly aware you would like.

The entries on the lists shown above are purposefully gentle and generic. Some of what excites you may be very personal and not for anyone but your partner to hear. As long as they are acceptable to both of you, add excitement, and dispel boredom, they'll get you back on track.

Step Six: How Will You Make Sure That Excitement Will Always Be Part of Your Relationship?

Excitement produces the capacity for more excitement, and boredom generates more apathy and irritability. You have the best chance of keeping your relationship exciting if you are in love with your own life and your partner feels the same.

If you are apathetic in other areas of your life, you will feel that way about your partner as well. If, on the other hand, you are excited about who you are personally, but consistently passive with your partner, the problem is more likely between the two of you. Defining where the problems are will help you to focus your energy where it's most needed.

Healing what has gone wrong is the first step. Ensuring that your relationship will continue to regenerate is another. You can make wonderful progress by doing the exercises together in this book, but you must make them a way of life. After all, promises are only as good as their delivery, and you must continue to invest the energy that quality maintenance requires.

You can make this transformation happen. The best goal is to become someone your partner is continually rediscovering because you are always in the process of transforming yourself. As a constantly evolving and emerging treasure, you will never be boring to yourself or your partner.

♥ EXERCISE: How I Intend to Stay an Exciting Person to Myself and to My Partner

By going through all of the above exercises, you now have a better understanding of how your relationship drifted from its initial excitement to its current lessened vitality. You and your partner have exchanged feelings and thoughts about what both of you have lost and what you need from each other to regain those delicious thrills that were once so spontaneous. This last exercise will help you focus on what you need to do to activate your own personal regeneration.

Make two lists. For the first list, write down what you feel are ten uninteresting things about yourself. They can be any of your thoughts, attitudes, values, and behaviors, ones that you would find boring or bothersome if you were dating yourself.

For the second list, write down ten characteristics that you find exciting about yourself and would be proud to share with someone you love.

Example

List One: Uninteresting things about me I'd like to leave behind.

- I incessantly worry about how I look.

- I am always late and upset about it.

- I'm compulsive about things being in order.

- I'm a little too controlling.

- I talk too much.

- I get upset over little things.

- I'm too defensive.

- I only listen to music and programs I like.

- I tend to resist change.

- I'm cranky when I first wake up.

List Two: Interesting and exciting things about me.

- I'm crazy about traveling.

- I'm really interested in people.

- I like tasting new foods.

- I'm really fun to be with when I'm relaxed.

- I love snuggling under the covers in the early morning.

- I'm very sensual.

- I'm always willing to say who I am and what I want.

- I'm confident but not too much.

- I don't stay upset very long.

- I can easily talk about how I feel.

Now ask yourself what you would be like if you could minimize your first list and maximize your second. Your partner may have different ideas about what he or she wants from you, but it is hard not to be excited by someone who likes who they are and isn't afraid to show it.

♥

Reflections

Excitement and boredom are two ends of a very complicated continuum. All relationships have their own rituals for security and permanence that couples rely on for comfort and stability. They are necessary for relationships to survive the bombardment of outside challenge and to deal with natural instabilities that come with relationship maturation.

But when comfort patterns take over and the partners become supporting characters in an uninteresting play, the pursuit of security and stability can destroy the very allure that brought them together. Couples who are willing to continually rewrite the script in an ever-intriguing way can make certain that a lack of excitement will never become a permanent part of their lives.

5

from *constructive challenges* to destructive conflicts

"Why does every disagreement become an argument?"

New lovers do have their challenges, but they are usually quick to resolve them to regain their intimacy. They are open to accepting the differences between them, because they want to avoid conflicts by minimizing their importance. Desiring to stay connected and live in a common reality, they search for ways to validate their lover's thoughts and feelings rather than challenge them.

> "As we get to know each other better, we know we won't always agree on everything, but it won't ever be a problem. We want to understand each other and accept the differences."

"I can't imagine anything he would see or feel that I wouldn't care about. He's the most fascinating person I've ever known."

"She sometimes drives me crazy with the odd way she looks at things, but when I really listen, she makes a lot of sense."

"I've learned so much from him about things I never understood and didn't even think I'd ever like. Now I realize how closed I was."

Even in fragile areas such as politics, religion, past relationships, and family skeletons, new lovers try to find a way to accommodate their partner's different ways of seeing the world. They don't want to erase their lover's realities or give up their own, so they enthusiastically search for ways to compromise.

As the Relationship Matures

As a relationship creates deeper intimacy and a more secure commitment, the partners feel freer to risk challenging the differences they once readily accepted. New conflicts that emerge face tougher standards for automatic approval.

Though most couples are willing to work at resolving the unexpected conflicts, the very presence of potential incompatibilities can strain the relationship in new and often unpredictable ways. Unresolved disagreements can turn prior lovers into verbal adversaries, resulting in the damage of their once secure and automatic support.

Eventually, the once deeply connected, impassioned debaters wonder if they can ever disagree again without ending up as enemies. Allergic to the process, they begin to anticipate there will be a painful outcome as soon as a controversy begins.

"I can see it coming before he's even aware. It's the expression on his face."

"She's winding up. I can feel it. She keeps telling me that nothing's wrong, but I know better. This is going to be ugly and there's nothing I can do to stop it."

"I don't even know why I try to talk to him about these sensitive subjects. I know what's going to happen, but I guess I just don't learn."

"Oh, great. I've got two choices: agree with her on something I don't believe in, or no sex for a week. Those are lousy options."

"Why can't we just talk about something and agree to disagree? Why does it always have to end up in a battle?"

If your unresolved conflicts have accumulated, you may find yourselves retreating behind well-established walls and less able to resolve your differences. Withholding your vulnerability from each other can result in feelings of helplessness, self-righteousness, hurt, and anger.

In order to maintain your love, you must not give in to that pattern of deteriorating interactions. You need to become more effective in your conflict resolution or you will risk sabotaging your chances of long-term success.

Is Your Relationship Suffering from Destructive Conflict?

- As you approach your partner to talk about something important, do you expect an argument?

- Do seemingly friendly disagreements often end up as painful battles?

- Are your arguments happening more frequently and repeatedly?

- After you've had an argument, does it take longer now to reconcile than it used to?

Many committed couples realize that their disagreements have gotten out of hand. Where they used to see each other as reasonable dissenters, they now experience each other as ever-ready challengers, poised to override any perceived opposition.

If you long for the time when you could say anything to each other, knowing you would be heard and respected, you will need to change your combative patterns and regain each other's trust.

♥ EXERCISE: Quick Check Combat Meter

Using the scoring system below, fill in the blanks with your corresponding point number. In your journal, write down any pertinent feelings or thoughts that may come to mind to share with each other later.

Eager to reconnect = 1

Somewhat upset but wanting to resolve things = 2

Only willing to resolve the conflict if he or she does too = 3

Needing my partner to come to me first and apologize = 4

Not willing to connect unless my partner admits he or she is wrong = 5

Too angry and discouraged to reconnect = 6

1. When my partner and I fight over little things, I am _____.

2. If my partner says something that hurts my feelings, I am _____.

3. When my partner obviously wants to win an argument, I am _____.

4. If my partner rejects me, I am _____.

5. If my partner gives me the silent treatment after a fight, I am _____.

6. When my partner and I can't solve a disagreement, I am _____.

7. If I know that I'm at fault in an argument, I am _____.

8. When I know that an argument has been unnecessary, I am _____.

9. When my partner tries to apologize, I am _____.

10. When my partner won't say he or she is wrong, I am _____.

Scoring

If your individual score is 20 or less, your relationship conflict is well within normal and not overly worrisome. If it is between 21 and 40, you're spending too much of your relationship energy in conflict. If your score is over 40, you risk relationship failure, and will need to start your healing plan as soon as possible.

♥

The Healing Plan

Your healing plan can take you back to the time when confrontation and challenge were stimulating and exciting, instead of resulting in righteous battles.

To achieve that goal, you will have to tear down any self-protective barriers you may have erected. The process may be painful at times, and will require humility, but the outcome is worth it.

Keep in mind that you once trusted your partner to respect your point of view even if he or she did not agree with it. Your mutual willingness to listen and to learn created an atmosphere of welcome. Your love for each other depended on the profound understanding that the beauty of your relationship was worth more than winning any argument. It's now time to re-create that openness.

Step One: Go Back to the Beginning of Your Relationship

You were once able to handle your differences without damaging your intimacy or losing respect for each other. You may have actually enjoyed some of those initial conflicts. They have perhaps increased your knowledge of each other.

In working through those early challenges, you learned your partner's triggers, the emotions behind them, and how to preserve your love for each other when the conflict was resolved. When you came back together, you felt a greater understanding of each other that may have brought you closer.

♥ EXERCISE: Early Disagreements and Their Resolutions

Many couples can remember their first fight, even when and where it occurred. They tell me how unsettled they were afterward, and how the despair of being so disconnected made them wonder if they really were soul mates after all. They worried, what if this fight was the beginning of a contentious pattern that would eventually destroy the relationship? When they were able to reconnect, they were incredibly grateful that their treasured intimacy had resurfaced.

The following exercise will help you remember those early times when disagreements were temporary disconnects that didn't permanently threaten your love, and even helped you to know each other better.

Write in your journal the first argument you can remember. Try to recall how you felt during the disagreement and what your feelings were when you intimately reconnected. Use the following questions to help guide your entries.

When you have finished, write a narrative that tells your partner what you remember about the situation. Ask if he or she remembers it and how the feelings were similar or different.

1. What was the argument about?

2. How early in your relationship did it occur?

3. What did you want from each other?

4. How did you resolve it?

5. Did you learn anything about your partner?

6. What emotions did you feel?

7. How long did it take you to reconnect?

8. Which of you was first to reconnect?

Example

"I totally remember our first argument because I was so upset. Looking back, I can see how ridiculous it seems, but I couldn't see it that way then.

"We'd been together only a few weeks. I wanted to spend the day with you just hanging out—you know—no plans. I thought you did too. Then your best friend called and said he needed to talk to you right away, some kind of crisis. I remember being really hurt and feeling rejected. I kind of blurted it out. You got angry and told me I was selfish.

"I thought you were making the wrong choice to choose him over us at the last minute. I remember stomping out of the house. I didn't get very far. I sat in the car realizing what I'd done.

"I remembered that one of the most beautiful things about you was how much you cared for the people you loved, and you would have done the same thing for me in a second. I felt so embarrassed and guilty for being so reactive and self-centered.

"I decided right then and asked you to forgive me. You took me in your arms and told me you were sorry for getting so angry and that you never meant to hurt me. I was so grateful."

♥

Suggestions

When you have each done this exercise, ask yourselves what helped you get over your disagreements so quickly when you were first in love. How did you change your behavior in order to get past them? What shifted that made that happen? Did you have to bury any emotions to get close again so soon, or did you actually let your negativity dissolve?

Share your responses with your partner and talk about the motivations you both used to make that reconciliation happen.

Step Two: Evaluate Your Current Relationship

All partners go through times when the frequency of their disagreements is affected by stressful situations, or times when they are more estranged from each other. It's natural for conflicts to ebb and flow as a relationship matures, but the need to handle them more effectively intensifies as your connection deepens.

If your conflicts have become unproductive, pervasive, and cumulatively hurtful, your relationship could be in danger. The next exercise will help you to identify what your current arguments are like and how you process them. Try to keep this in a spirit of inquiry, to see if you can better understand each other's distresses as you talk about these contentious interactions.

♥ EXERCISE: Our Current Disagreements

In your journal, list the three most frequently repeated arguments you have with your partner. Write a short narrative about each one to read to your partner when you have completed the exercise.

Using the following questions as your guide, be as honest as you can, even if you feel you may be activating your partner's opposition. To heal your argumentative relationship, you must first understand your differences without judging or invalidating each other's experience.

1. What am I asking from my partner that I'm not getting?

2. What are my reasons for continuing to argue about this?

3. What is my approach when we argue?

4. What is my partner's typical response?

5. What happens as a result of our interaction?

6. How do I feel when it's over?

Example

"I desperately want you to get off the damn computer at night so we can have more time together. I feel as if I'm competing with your online intrigue, and I'm losing. I keep bringing it up, hoping that I will change your mind, which is obviously stupid.

"I guess I keep pushing, wanting so much for you to eventually get how important this is to me. You keep telling me that you agree, and after each argument, you're better for a while. Then it starts all over again. I realize I start the arguments, but I try to hold it back as long as I can and then I come out swinging.

"After I attack, you start making your list of legitimate excuses and then blame me for being too demanding. Then I feel guilty, like I'm too needy or something, and I cave. Same deal. I know it'll happen again and I don't know what to do about my frustration."

♥

Suggestions

When you've finished writing your three examples, take turns reading each of them to each other. The disagreements may be the same or different, but whoever is listening must not defend or argue.

After you have listened to each example, remember to validate your partner's right to feel however he or she does. You don't have to agree or even see things the same way, but you must respect and support your partner's reality, whether it is the same as yours or not. Your goal is to understand each other's cumulative frustration.

Step Three: When Did You Begin to Drift?

Couples rarely notice the subtle changes they experience when their prior debates slip into competitive arguments. Many conflicts begin as small differences and grow more dangerous over time. Others arise because of unexpected demands, outside pressures, or traumas, and may strike without warning.

Your destructive-conflict interactions likely did not happen overnight. Go back in time and take note of when you began to grow less patient and more easily frustrated with your partner. You may only have noticed because you had let things go so many times before and felt you could not do it again. Those cumulative small resentments that you'd buried in the past can easily account for the quickness to irritability you may be suffering now.

In the following exercise, try to help each other remember when your feelings began to change and how you responded. These memories may be loaded with long-buried feelings that can arouse defensiveness. Go easy with each other as you dig into past vulnerabilities.

♥ EXERCISE: Your First Memories of Intolerance

Some people can actually remember a single event where they snapped at a partner in a new way, but most repeated unproductive altercations happen slowly over time, where the original experience has blended into many others.

In the following exercise, try to recall one or more interactions with your partner where you became aware that your tolerance was diminishing and your negative reactions were much stronger.

Using as much detail as you can, write down where you were, what was happening at the time, and why you think you felt less patient and more critical than before. What did you dislike about your partner's behavior, and what might have been going on in your own life that influenced your reaction?

You may not be able to recall an exact time when your feelings and responses began to change. That's okay. At some time that difference occurred. Try to remember how those feelings developed during the several events that could have tipped the balance.

Example

"I remember the exact time when I couldn't listen to one more excuse from you about why you spent money on something we hadn't agreed on.

"It was that summer when we made a deal to save everything for our Christmas trip. We promised each other that we'd hold back from buying anything we didn't absolutely need, and I started taking on extra work to make sure we'd have enough. You knew I was exhausted.

"Then you show up with one of those new expensive, powered wave skimmers. Sure, your friend wanted to dump it and said you could pay him when you had the money. What money? I felt so betrayed. Your word about working with me on the budget means nothing to me anymore. We've been arguing about money ever since, and we'll never agree.

"I've tried to resolve this in every way I know how, even offering to keep my money separate so you could do what you want with yours. You just blow up and get angrier at me. I've just about given up, but it affects everything else in our relationship. I still love you, but this conflict tears me apart. I just can't trust you anymore."

♥

Suggestions

When you share these past moments of distress with your partner, you may feel frustration and resentment. Please don't let those feelings negatively affect your goals. Your goal is to discover how you changed from welcome challengers to angry adversaries.

Step Four: What Stopped You from Resolving Your Differences When They Happened?

Because of positive interactions that partners want to retain, they often don't recognize emerging conflicts as significant threats. By the time they notice that their arguments are happening more often and with less resolution, they may already be less able to fully rebound between them.

When you recall those earlier disagreements in an attempt to understand why you let things go or didn't try to resolve those increasing conflicts, please don't blame yourself or your partner. Like so many other people, you may not realize how, over time, negative interactions can create more damage than positives can compensate for. Or you may have felt confident that you and your partner knew just how far you could push things before permanent damage occurred, but then miscalculated. Without your realizing it, your cumulative unresolved interactions had secretly stolen your relationship's resilience.

♥ EXERCISE: What Could I Have Done Differently to Resolve Our Conflict?

This is an exercise in self-accountability that should be done independently from your partner. It is very human to want to place blame on your partner when something goes wrong between you, but admitting your own part in any conflict is the first step in genuine resolution. It is well worth it to accept whatever you contributed to the problem if it helps you gain insight and the power to change.

Recall any repeated argument between you and your partner. Use an example of one that has become more uncomfortable for both of you as your relationship has matured. Note everything you can imagine about what your partner may have needed during your argument, and how important the outcome may have been to him or her.

In your journal, write down how that interaction usually plays out by creating a simulated dialogue. Keep it brief or reasonable in length so as not to overload your partner when you exchange your exercises.

Next, create a new dialogue for the same argument, but one with a better resolution that brings you closer after it is over. Stay as open and as emotionally generous as you can. Your partner should do the same.

Example

First Dialogue

Your partner:	"Could we do something more interesting this weekend than usual?"
You:	"You have all the time in the week to do what you want. I've been working all week. I want to watch the games. You know how important they are."
Your partner:	"I have plenty of responsibilities all week. I keep this house running. I get bored. You don't have to watch every damn game on TV."
You:	"Call one of your friends or something. I'm not responsible for your excitement in life."
Your partner:	"That's sure not the way you feel when you want something."
You:	"Don't pull that guilt trip on me. Plan something for late Sunday if it's so important."
Your partner:	"The day is over by then. I want to do something with you when we have more time."
You:	"Football season will be over soon. You can figure something out until then, okay?"

Result: Distance and resentment.

Example

Second Dialogue

Your partner: "Could we do something more interesting this
                  weekend than usual?"

You: "I know you're stuck around the house all week,
                  honey, but there are some important football games
                  on this weekend and I really want to watch them."

Your partner: "Do you have to watch every game?"

You: "No, I just look forward to them. You really want
                  to get out this weekend, huh?"

Your partner: "I've just felt so cooped up, and I miss being with
                  you and going on an adventure. Like we used to,
                  remember?"

You: (laughing) "Can I bring the portable radio?"

Your partner: (smiling) "Only to hear the scores once every hour,
                  okay?"

You: "Deal. Does that mean sex later?"

Your partner: (teasing) "How about listening every two hours?"

Result: Compromise, resolution, and intimacy.

♥

Suggestions

When disagreements uncover genuine incompatibilities, the partners in a loving relationship can still share their feelings and know they will at least be welcomed. They may have to agree to disagree, but neither need hurt the other in the process. Invalidation, guilt, bullying, and blame are effective ways to win an argument. They're also guaranteed to cause separation, cumulative emotional distance, and the destruction of intimacy.

Step Five: What Do You Need from Each Other to Heal Your Destructive Conflicts?

No relationship is without conflict. All couples disagree from time to time, whether those controversies are minimal or significant. True harmony comes from the successful resolution of differences, not from their absence. Couples who approach their differences with respect and mutual support are more likely to find creative solutions that will incorporate the best of both of their opinions.

The difference between healthy and unhealthy conflict is determined by two things: the way the partners interact during the conflict and whether or not the interaction produces a mutually favorable outcome. If your arguments are repetitive, angry, and blaming, they will eventually outweigh whatever good exists between you. On the other hand, if you challenge each other with the intent for positive change and do so with loving support, you will handle future conflicts in ever more effective ways.

♥ EXERCISE: Healthy and Unhealthy Conflicts

The purpose of this exercise is to help you recognize the difference between healthy and unhealthy conflicts and to stop destructive arguments before they do damage.

In your journal, write two lists. The first list will consist of five conflicts that you and your partner repeat on a regular basis. Choose those that you have never been able to adequately resolve and that have always left you more frustrated and emotionally distant. The second list will consist of five conflicts you resolved in a way that brought you closer to each other, leaving you more confident that you would be able to handle future disagreements.

With each of your examples, write a short narrative using the following questions to help you remember. When you are done writing, you'll want to take turns sharing the entries on both lists with your partner.

When did the conflict occur?

What led up to it?

What was the disagreement about?

How did you feel when you were arguing?

What ended the argument?

Did anything get resolved?

If so, what?

Did you feel closer or more distant afterward?

Do you believe that the same argument will happen again?

Example

From List One

"My most frustrating, repeated argument with you is the one we have about our sex life. I know you like sex often and don't really need the kind of romantic buildup that I do. You keep telling me I should be more like you, but I need more connection before I can really get into it.

"I used to look forward to making love, but now I more often feel like I'm just a means to an end. I try to get you to listen before it becomes an issue again, but you won't. I can tell that it's going to come up every time we haven't had sex for a few days.

"You keep telling me how frustrated you are, and I keep telling you how lonely I feel, but we never seem to get anywhere. We end up mad and distant. Then, when we finally have sex again, we're not really lovers, we're just using our sexual connection to avoid feeling the heartache between us.

"I don't ever want to argue about this again, but I don't know what to do. I'm worried that we'll destroy the sex we do enjoy."

From List Two

"I recall an argument we used to have all the time and how we finally were able to get it totally resolved. It was about how much we would each contribute financially to our life together, remember? I was making more money than you at the time. You didn't want to take advantage of me, and I wanted you to. It makes me smile to remember how much we cared about each other's feelings.

"You'd fought so hard for your own financial independence and you were proud of it. I didn't want to take that away from you, but I wanted a lifestyle for both of us that you couldn't afford on your own.

"Remember that final day when we just decided to do a percentage split? We couldn't understand why we hadn't thought of that before. You were so excited to do the spreadsheet that made it all so clear. We never argued about it again, and loved each other more for it."

♥

Suggestions

The goal of this exercise is to leave behind unproductive conflicts that undermine your love and destroy your faith in your ability to resolve your differences. You won't be able to stop disagreeing, nor should you expect to. You also won't be able to solve every conflict the way you would like to, but you can agree to disagree without withholding love as a punishment.

Unfortunately, there are some incompatibilities that cannot be resolved, and the partners in a relationship must agree to let them go or risk losing each other. Those decisions are painful and hard to make. It may be helpful to seek professional help if unresolved conflicts are stopping you from moving ahead.

Step Six: How to Effectively Resolve Future Conflicts

I often observe couples in their counseling sessions get into long-standing, repeated, and destructive conflicts. They seem to be helplessly caught up in their self-created traumatic interaction. This appears to serve no purpose except to exchange pent-up anger and gain retribution.

When they finally complete each emotional battle, they are often embarrassed, realizing that their behavior has not only appeared stupid and ineffective, but has not resolved anything. They feel terrible, but they don't know what else to do with their overwhelming frustration and hopelessness.

If both partners are open to changing their patterns, I often suggest the following exercise before we begin delving into their reasons for their continuous embattlements:

"Please face each other. Look into each other's eyes and hold hands. Be absolutely silent for five minutes. During that time, imagine that, were you to have this fight one more time, it would be the final time you would see each other as long as you live. If so, what would you be willing to do to keep that from happening?"

How the couple responds is, in itself, telling. When the outcome is hopeful, they appear to readily understand how much they are risking by participating in these useless, repetitive, irresolvable battles. A miracle moment occurs between them where they look at each other with deep sadness and understand what they have been risking. I know then they have a chance to resolve their process and bring themselves back together.

If the couple fails to be reflective and sobered after they complete the exercise, they often resume their impotent rage, fighting now over why the other didn't do the process well enough or how meaningless it was. If that happens, their relationship has a much slimmer chance of working.

You can do this same exercise together, and you can repeat it whenever you are in danger of slipping into your old destructive patterns. What would your feelings be if you and your partner had to face an irrevocable end to your relationship because of your continued bickering? Would that deter your need to continue in the same pattern? The risks you are taking are real, and that despairing ending could actually happen.

To ensure that your relationship has the chance of leaving destructive conflicts behind, you must be able to predict them, understand their significantly negative potential, agree to disengage from them when they threaten, and practice a better way of resolving them.

♥ EXERCISE: Predicting Destructive Conflicts

In your journal, write down the physical, emotional, and psychological warning signs that signal that a destructive conflict is on its way. Incorporate them into a simple narrative that you can share with your partner.

Negative potentials are what you both know in your hearts will linger on long after your disagreement ends. These are especially destructive when they endlessly repeat. Somewhere, in the unseen labyrinths of your relationship, they will fester and make each succeeding negative interaction worse.

Example

Recognizing the signs

"I can always tell when we're going to have a fight. We get short with each other and a little sarcastic. My stomach starts to knot up and I feel helpless, like we're on the edge of an emotional cascade and there's nothing I can do to stop us from going over the edge. I want to reach out and reassure you, but you seem so distant. It's as if I don't know you. I wish I could reconnect at those times, but I don't know how."

Example

Understanding the Negative Potential

"I know this fight is going to set us back for a week. It always ends up in a terrible heartbreak for both of us. We've been arguing about this for so long and we never have been able to make it better. I know it's hurting our relationship and we are treading on thin ice. If this doesn't get any better, we'll end up apart. I'm sick inside and really worried I'm going to lose you if we can't find a way out."

Example

Making Agreements for Better Resolutions

"I want to get past this. I love you and don't want to hurt you anymore. I don't want to continue feeling the pain of your anger and resentment. I'm willing to do whatever I can to change these interactions and to resolve our conflict once and for all. Please work with me to get beyond our repeated, destructive conflicts and to be my friend again. We were a great team once. We can be again.

"Maybe we can't do everything right, but we can go a long way to make things better. I want to be open and vulnerable with you, and I want you to feel the same way with me. Let's work together and create solutions that we both can embrace. I love you too much to let these differences drive us apart."

♥

Suggestions

These honest and vulnerable offerings must be received with the same caring and openness as they are given. The feelings and evaluations of how important any one conflict is may be different for each partner. It is not important that they be the same. What counts is the respect each partner gives to the other's experience.

Reflections

Of all the stumbles that relationships endure, slipping into destructive, repeated, irresolvable conflicts can cause the most damage.

When relationships are new, partners seem to thrive on the excitement of resolving differences. It is the most significant way they can learn about each other. Their negative passion of temporary disconnection is eclipsed by the thrill of reuniting.

For whatever reasons, many partners fall prey over time to seeing each other's desires as mutually exclusive threats to their own. The conflicts that were once stimulating and expanding become angry separations and wear away at their love.

Fortunately, these destructive battles are not only healable, but their transformation can create a new way of being for both partners. They'll be able to be honest without being hurtful and open without being invalidated. Holding emotional hands, they can look forward to helping each other change from adversaries to allies.

from **sacrificing** **for your partner** to *self-preservation*

"I can't always put you first anymore."

If you have known the exquisite experience of new love, you will remember the delicious openness, unconditional welcoming, and sweet fusion you so enjoyed. Your loved one's every need and desire so easily became yours to fulfill and their happiness was your greatest reward.

When your lover was your greatest treasure, you were willing and able to put your own needs aside. You felt your partner's happiness or sorrow more deeply than you felt your own. Exulting in his or her comfort, you wanted to grant every desire and prevent any sorrow.

> "She's on a trip to Europe with her friends, going to places she's never been before. I find myself thinking of her every minute, wondering if she's okay."

"I know he sometimes forgets to eat when he's busy. When I'm enjoying a meal with someone else, I always wonder if he's hungry."

"I knew she went to sleep without remembering to fill her gas tank. I was still up, so I thought I'd drive over there and take care of it, just to make sure she'd be okay in the morning."

"He works such long hours, but I never mind waiting for him, no matter how late it is. I can always find something to do until I'm in his arms again."

These caring, spontaneously generous moments seem so easy when love is new. Your motivation to please is ever-regenerating, and your lover's appreciative smile is all you need in return. Generosity begets reciprocal generosity, allowing both of you to bask in the comfort of self-indulgence without embarrassment. This easy exchange of desire and fulfillment is so basic to new love that anything less would seem unnatural.

As the Relationship Matures

Your motivation to sacrifice unconditionally understandably lessened as your relationship matured. You hopefully continued to be concerned about your partner's well-being, though you realized you couldn't be expected to sacrifice your own needs in every situation, no matter how strong your devotion. Were you to have forever sacrificed at the expense of your own self-preservation, you would have put yourself at risk of feeling exploited by the person you had trusted the most.

From Generosity to Keeping Score

New love can mask your need for self-preservation and allow you to give too much, hoping your partner will recognize the imbalance and correct it. Basking in the joy of your indulgence, he or she may not notice.

Abandoned and resentful, you may find yourself beginning to keep score, carefully comparing the number of favors you are exchanging. The initial generosity that once existed between the two of you will significantly diminish, and your love for each other will suffer proportionately.

Have You Begun Putting Yourself Ahead of Your Partner?

If you have allowed your generosity to get out of balance and are already keeping score, you will have to right that balance. Please do not criticize yourself. You most likely believed that there would always be enough love to go around and that you both would always be fair.

If the balance between taking care of yourself and nurturing your partner has shifted, you may feel conflicted. You never wanted to let your partner down or feel that you had to withhold your generosity to protect yourself. Your slide from pleasing your partner to taking care of yourself probably went unnoticed until it became obvious that things were out of balance.

♥ EXERCISE: Quick Check Care Meter

The following set of questions will help you and your partner evaluate how much you have drifted from the spontaneous generosity you felt when your love was new. Using the following scoring system, fill in the blank with the point value that corresponds to your answer.

I am still very willing to sacrifice = 1

I am somewhat willing but need recognition = 2

I am willing only if I'm convinced that the request is reasonable = 3

I often feel that the request is inappropriate and will only comply if I get something in return = 4

I am resentful but will do it out of obligation = 5

I often don't feel like giving anything anymore = 6

1. When my partner asks for something I don't particularly like doing, _____.

2. If I'm doing something for myself, and my partner needs something right away, _____.

3. If I'm feeling stressed and my partner wants me to care for him or her, _____.

4. When my partner asks me to change my plans, _____.

5. When I want something and my partner wants something different, _____.

6. When I feel neglected and my partner wants to be taken care of instead, _____.

7. If my partner says he or she needs me, but I'm tired of always being the one who gives, _____.

♥

Scoring

If each of you has a score between 7 and 14, it means you are caring well for each other. If your scores are between 15 and 28, you've accumulated underlying resentment and need to talk about it. If you both scored over 29, your relationship needs healing to restore a healthier balance of giving.

The Healing Plan

The goal of your healing plan is to regain the spontaneous generosity you once had for each other, while simultaneously being more realistic about making sure your own needs are met.

Step One: Go Back to the Beginning of Your Relationship

Your initial love of giving to each other, as sweet as it felt, was skewed in the direction of too much self-sacrifice. Because your motivation was so intense, you may have felt comfortable in that overgenerous exchange. As your relationship matured, your desire to be so generous has understandably diminished.

At the same time, remember that those original feelings were genuine. The joy of granting each other's every wish was both real and deeply satisfying. A better balance between caring for your partner and taking care of yourself can bring back the joy you once knew, while allowing you to be more reasonable in your expectations of yourself and your partner.

♥ EXERCISE: The Love of Giving

In your journal, write down several incidents when you were newly in love where you remember gladly going out of your way to please your partner. Try to recall those where you willingly sacrificed your own needs. When you have written them down, write a narrative to explain your feelings to your partner.

Example

"We met during that freezing winter in New York. Your little apartment never got warm. You'd linger in the shower just to postpone the shock of the cold air when you came out. I remember the first time I came back from the laundry room with that big warm towel and wrapped it around you as you got out. You told me that no one had ever cared for you that way, even as a child. I assured you it made me happier than it did you.

"It got a little harder to get down to the dryer when I worked late and the mornings came too soon. I had to set the alarm to make sure I got up in time, but I never wanted you to be cold again. The summer would come soon enough, and the sacrifice was well worth it."

Example

"I always preferred making love at night so we could fall asleep in each other's arms, but you told me one night that you always felt sexier in the morning. I've been a morning sleepwalker all my life, but I knew how important it was to you, and you hardly asked for anything from me. Sometimes I had to get up an hour early just to shower and get a cup of coffee into me before I could function. I never woke you, just snuggled back in bed in time. You seemed so happy. I knew it was right."

When you've each written your examples, read them aloud to each other. Ask your partner to go back in time with you and to remember those moments. Share what you feel as you reexperience them together.

♥

Suggestions

These shared experiences can unearth deep emotions. They may feel bittersweet if you feel less giving toward each other in your current relationship. Please stay with the feelings and don't allow any present sadness to stop you from remembering the sweetness that once was.

Step Two: Evaluate Your Current Relationship

You should not expect your current relationship to have the same level of generosity you felt when your love was new. You were focusing only on each other then, bathing in the delight of new discoveries and infrequent conflict. Even so, you most probably still do kind and caring things for each other, even if less often.

In the following two exercises, you'll list some of the ways you still put your partner's needs above your own, and the times you now choose your own needs instead.

However your relationship has changed, please don't feel bad about your current priorities. It is easy to find fault when you compare the past to the present. Resist pointing out your partner's self-preserving priorities or making excuses for your own. Your goal is to simply examine how your behaviors have changed.

♥ EXERCISE: How I Currently Sacrifice Myself for My Partner

In your journal, write three behaviors you regularly do for your partner that are clearly sacrifices on your part.

Choose those offerings that you make without resentment or martyrdom. When you have written them down, write a narrative to your partner using the following questions to guide you:

Did my partner realize I was sacrificing my needs for him or her?

How important do I think my sacrifice is?

What do I think my partner feels when I put his or her needs above my own?

How would my partner feel if I took care of myself instead?

When you've written your narratives, share them with your partner. Ask him or her about any differences you may feel about your choices, and compare your thoughts. Then ask your partner to do the same.

The goal of this exercise is to see if your partner has noted and appreciated your current sacrifices. If you succeeded, your gift will easily compensate for your sacrifice. If not, it would be a better choice the next time around to only make those sacrifices if your partner enjoys and appreciates them.

Example

"I get up early on the weekends to feed our animals so that you can sleep in. I know you love them as much as I do, but it's really hard for you to start the day that way.

"I don't look forward to that responsibility either, especially early in the morning, but I know that it doesn't bother me as much as it would you, and I like to take care of your needs and see you smile when you awaken.

"I think you realize that I am willingly sacrificing for you and that you are grateful, but you don't say anything about it. I also know you would do it for me if I asked. I'd love to know if it is as important to you as I think it is, and if you believe I care for you when I do it. I would love to feel your appreciation if it were real, but I don't want to pressure you. I'm not sure how you would respond if I stopped giving that to you."

♥

♥ EXERCISE: When I Sacrifice My Partner's Needs for My Own

Now write in your journal three behaviors where you consistently put your own needs over your partner's. Choose examples where you are aware that your partner would probably prefer you to sacrifice, but you still prioritize your own needs.

When you have written them down, write a narrative to your partner using the following questions to guide you:

What is the behavior?

What made me choose my own needs over my partner's in this case?

Does my partner seem aware that I'm making that choice?

What do I think my partner is feeling when I do this?

What are my feelings about my choice?

When you have written your narratives, share them with your partner. Ask if he or she feels the same way as you do about your choices, and compare your thoughts. Then ask your partner to do the same.

Your goal is to understand how your partner responds to your choices. It may be that you are feeling guilt unnecessarily or are causing greater hurt than you intend. Awareness gives you the option to willingly take the consequences or to choose differently if you wish.

Example

"I know you take care of the kids all week when I'm at work and would really appreciate it if I took care of them on Saturday mornings so you could have some time to yourself. My conflict is that it's the only morning my buddies get together to play basketball and hang out afterward. I look forward to spending that time with them. I'm only gone a few hours, but it regenerates me for the rest of the weekend.

"I've asked you to get a sitter so you can take some time off too, but you choose to be with the kids instead. I wonder sometimes if you do that just to make me feel guilty. I tell you I'll take care of them in the afternoon, but you say it's too late in the day for you to do anything meaningful. I feel guilty as hell, but I guess I don't trust you to make sure I get what I need."

♥

Suggestions

Sharing what you have written could generate feelings of anger or resentment. Please don't allow any negative feelings to interfere with what you're trying to learn about each other. You may find that most of what you share won't come as a surprise, but having it out in the open will give you options for change.

Step Three: When Did You Begin to Shift?

You didn't change from putting your partner's needs over your own to self-preservation overnight, and it was probably not a smooth transition. The demands for the energy and resources that fuel sacrificial giving change with life's stressors. You may not have realized that you altered your priorities until a significant event occurred that uncovered your new choices.

♥ EXERCISE: Remembering the First Time I Didn't Put My Partner's Needs Over My Own

In your journal, write about the first time you can remember taking care of yourself at the expense of your partner's needs. Choose an example that was an unexpected departure from the past. Use the following questions as a guide to help you write the narrative to share with your partner later:

What was the situation?

What would my partner have expected from my behavior in the past?

What were my conflicting needs?

What was my partner's response when I didn't respond as I have in the past?

What did I feel?

What happened in our relationship as a result of my choice?

When you have finished your part of the exercise, ask your partner to do the same.

Example

"I remember the situation exactly and still feel terrible about it after all this time. I was out with my buddies at that World Series game I'd looked forward to for weeks. You and I weren't getting along well—we had this stupid ongoing argument about your twin sister's constant interference in our lives. I just remember being a little pissed off, and not feeling much like sacrificing for you as I would have before.

"I know I sounded irritated when you called me and told me you needed me to come home. I wasn't in the mood to be concerned about you when I was having a great time. I think I told you it had better be for a good reason.

"You started crying and told me you couldn't talk and you really needed me. I said I wasn't going to leave the game unless I thought it was important. You said you couldn't talk because your sister was listening and that if I really cared I wouldn't ask. I wouldn't take no for an answer and pushed you for more information, but you hung up.

"I was angry at your reaction, but I guess you had a right. I'd never done anything like this before, but I was fed up always being there for you. When I came home, you'd left to go to the police station to help your sister file a report. You left a note saying that something terrible had happened to her and you didn't expect me to understand or feel any compassion because of the way I felt about her.

"When you called from the hospital and told me about the attack, I felt terrible and apologized profusely, but you'd pulled away and didn't seem to care. I showed up to help, but you wouldn't talk to me and I didn't blame you.

"We got through it somehow, but you never really forgave me. I know it started a downward spiral where we started withholding from each other."

♥

Suggestions

Your partner may not remember the incidents that stand out in your mind, or wouldn't give them the same importance. Something that seems insignificant to one person can be a milestone to another, and many small slights can easily lead up to bigger disappointments.

You want to know each other more deeply, and contrasting those memories will give both of you a chance. Ask your partner to listen without judgment, and be certain to offer the same in return.

Step Four: What Stopped You from Confronting the Situation When You First Began to Withhold?

Small disappointments are easily eclipsed by life's understandable demands, and their cumulative effects are not always recognized until they become a problem. As new love's generosity gives way to more individual priorities, most couples don't realize they are changing.

If your relationship has suffered because of your lessened giving, then your current interaction is not working and you will have to negotiate a better one. Learning what happened in the past will help you do that and also help you identify warning signs in the future.

♥ EXERCISE: What Stopped You from Healing the Rift?

Using one of your own examples of when you sacrificed your partner's needs in favor of your own, write down what was going on in your relationship at the time. Describe what kept you from healing the growing rift between you. Include the following areas in your narrative.

How were you feeling about your relationship at the time?

What got in your way of healing the imbalance?

Did you try to talk to your partner about your feelings?

What was your partner's response?

Could you have done anything different at the time?

When you have finished, read these narratives out loud to each other. Look for overlapping feelings and those that are different. You're using these exercises to learn to live in the heart and mind of your partner. You will feel more compassion for each other if you can feel your partner's distresses as well as your own.

Example

"I was unhappy with you when I made that choice to pull away and take care of my own needs. You'd been working late every night for weeks, and you seemed totally preoccupied with what was important to you. When I tried to share little things with you, you didn't seem interested. I was putting out huge amounts of energy to keep everything else going. You know what I mean: friends, family, house, bills, personal stuff—every aspect of our relationship.

"I know I agreed to help you build the business, but I guess it was just too much for me. I figured that I'd better take care of myself because you sure weren't going to. I realize now I could have talked to you about how sad I was, but you seemed so cranky and out of reach.

"Staying out of your way was the only thing I knew how to do, so I did things without you. I wish I'd tried harder to share my feelings with you and not let us get so far apart."

♥

Suggestions

This exercise will have better results if you focus on your own accountability. It is often tempting to reverse the blame when you are feeling remorse for your own decisions. Assume that both of you had good reasons to make the choices you did at the time.

Step Five: What Do You Need from Each Other Now?

This step will be the most important for you to heal this stumble. In the following exercise, you'll be working to regain the joy of giving without paying the price of sacrificing your own needs. That process will require both of you to be:

- Honest about what you want from your partner

- Clear about what you can give

- In agreement as to what is fair

- Committed to holding to your contract

- Willing to renegotiate if you feel a need for change

♥ EXERCISE: A Workable Contract

Write as many as ten significant needs you currently do not receive. This may not be a guarantee that you will get them now, but expressing them will make it more likely and may open up acceptable new alternatives. Use the following list as guide.

Example

I need to be touched in some way every day.

I need you to speak gently and lovingly to me when you feel critical.

I need you to recognize my sexual needs without my having to remind you.

I need you to stop drinking so much.

I need you to take care of your health.

I need you to be willing to celebrate special occasions.

I need you to keep your promises.

I need you to be more forgiving when I make a mistake.

I need time to myself.

I need more excitement.

When each of you has written down your needs, read them aloud to each other. Answer each of your partner's needs with one of the following responses and then ask for his or her thoughts and feelings:

Generosity:

I can give that to you without resentment.

Reciprocity:

I can give that to you, but I need _____ in return.

Bargaining:

I can give _____ to you, but not _____ .

Exchange:

I can't give you that, but instead I'm willing to offer _____ .

♥

Suggestions

Remember, you are sharing these intimate needs with each other to better understand what you can freely give and what you cannot. Your needs and availabilities may not always overlap, but your honesty and willingness to learn about each other's needs will make them more likely to be granted.

Step Six: Safeguarding Your Relationship

In order to maintain a balanced relationship between giving and self-care, both of you must be willing to make joint decisions about priorities and your use of common resources.

For that to happen, you will need to regain trust that you can gauge the importance of each other's needs as you once did. Knowing how to help each other recognize and express those vulnerabilities will give you back the unique connection you have lost. You are not obligated to fulfill your partner's every need, but it will make both of you feel more cared for just to recognize that those needs exist.

♥ EXERCISE: The Sweetness of Being Known

This exercise is to help you renew your ability to know each other's needs and evaluate their importance.

Pick one significant present desirse that would make you feel as treasured as when your love was new. It can be for a single behavior or a more overall change. Create a narrative explaining your desire in your most vulnerable terms. Using the scale below, rate that desire from 1 to 4.

Somewhat important = 1

Important = 2

Significantly important = 3

Crucially important = 4

Without telling your partner the level of importance ahead of time, share your desire narrative and ask your partner to guess its importance to you on the same scale. Then share any feelings you may have about the request and whether you would both agree to make it happen.

Then reverse the process.

Example

"I want you to share more of your inner thoughts with me. I so much want to know you better, and I'm always trying to guess what matters to you and what doesn't. I love your strength and your composure, but I need to know where you're vulnerable, too. I want to feel more needed and trusted.

"I don't know if you purposefully withhold, or that's just your nature, or if you'll even make the time to share your thoughts with me. Please tell me how you feel about this, and let me know if I can do anything to make it easier for you. I so much look forward to feeling closer to you."

♥

Suggestions

The most important thing about this exercise is to practice sensitivity, respect, and nonjudgment about any request either of you may have.

Remember, neither of you may be able to grant every wish regardless of its importance. Still, going through the exercise will help you become more attuned to each other's needs should you wish to grant them at some other time.

Reflections

The balance between caring for self and caring for the one you love must be trustworthy and fair. No one can keep giving forever if he or she feels continuously taken advantage of. Similarly, no loving partner should expect to be continually indulged at the expense of the other.

Accurately communicating your desires does not guarantee they will be fulfilled, but knowing the importance of each other's needs will help you make the best decisions together. It may not always be easy to watch over your partner's needs at the same time as your own, but if both of you are committed to doing that for each other, you will succeed.

from **being a team**
to *operating solo*

"We used to do everything together. Now I handle most of my challenges without you."

Most new lovers will eventually face misunderstandings, unantici-pated discoveries, and differences in rhythm and desire. If they team up together to solve those challenges, they can blend their individual resources, diminish their problems, and multiply their blessings.

"When she needs me, I'm there. I don't care how irrational it may seem at the moment. If she's got a problem, I've got a problem."

"When he's up against something that upsets him, I'll do anything I can to make it easier for him. He's got enough on his plate."

"She's this sounding board for any unhappy person within a five-mile radius. God bless her, I love her heart, but she gets so tired and still can't seem to say no. Even though it's not easy for her, we're working to get her free from so many obligations because they get in the way of our time together."

"I know he's really young to have such high cholesterol. It's kind of a pain to have to be so careful when we cook meals together, but it's not his fault and I want him to be okay forever."

"Living so far from each other is a pain for both of us, but it doesn't really matter as long as we eventually can find a way to be together all the time. It's not a serious problem compared to the great relationship we have."

New lovers don't have to think about whether they should help each other. They have a ready willingness to join together to solve any important issue, confident they can handle problems better together than they could by themselves.

As the Relationship Matures

As your attachment deepens, you and your partner, confident in the security of your commitment, will begin to reestablish your independence from each other. Handling other priorities you have neglected when you were newly in love, you may no longer feel as obligated or interested in automatically doing everything with your partner.

Initiation Becomes Passivity

Drifting from the closeness you counted upon in the past, you may have become less available to each other without realizing it. It's easy to begin focusing on personal priorities when your partner seems preoccupied with his or her own involvements. Without even realizing it, you may have undermined the team you both once counted upon.

Or you may be alone in your desire to stay a team while your partner has redirected his or her focus to other priorities. If that is so, you may be feeling abandoned and confused, wondering why your mutual devotion has diminished. If you are experiencing those feelings, it is always best to express your disappointment, rather than retreat or hope your partner will notice on his or her own. If you don't try whatever you can to repair the rift, you may risk drifting farther apart.

Has Your Relationship Become a Parallel Partnership?

If you now handle most of your problems without reaching out to your partner for help, you may have given up expecting the team support you once had. You're likely to be harboring resentment or emotionally disconnecting to avoid the sadness of rejection. Or perhaps you rationalize your feelings of abandonment by convincing yourself that you can cope just as well alone.

There is, hopefully, a "red telephone" in every committed relationship, no matter how parallel the partners have become. In traumatic situations, most partners resurrect their initial team support mode to take care of the situation at hand, even if the automatic devotion they once felt has diminished.

♥ EXERCISE: Quick Check Solo Meter

The following set of questions will help you and your partner evaluate how much you have drifted from being a team to operating solo. Using the following scoring system, fill in the blank with the point number that corresponds to your answer.

Most often available and on board = 1

Willingly available if the problem is important to my partner = 2

Only available if the situation seems legitimate to me = 3

Available when I don't have other, more important
priorities = 4

Available only when I'm pushed, when I get something for
it, or when the benefit is too good to refuse = 5

Not interested in helping unless there's no other alternative
= 6

1. When my partner needs my support, I am _____.

2. When my partner is suffering from a situation that is not as
    important to me, I am _____.

3. When my partner could do something on his or her own but
    asks me to do it instead, I am _____.

4. If my partner springs a need on me without letting me know in
    advance, I am _____.

5. If my partner is in real trouble, I am _____.

6. If my partner hasn't been there for me but still needs my help,
    I am _____.

7. If my partner needs me, but I don't think the problem is that
    important, I am _____.

8. If my partner keeps asking me for something that seems irrel-
    evant, I am _____.

Scoring

If your individual score is 8 to 16, you're very available to your
partner and in a partnership that still operates as a team. If your
score is between 17 and 32, your availability is conditional even
when your partner is distressed. If your score is 33 or higher, your
automatic support for each other is in the danger zone.

♥

The Healing Plan

To trust each other's willingness to participate as a team again, you'll need to understand how and why you turned away from that interdependent partnership. The multiple interactions that took you away from each other may have happened at different times and in different ways. To begin your healing process, you need to first examine how you worked together when your love was new.

Step One: Go Back to the Beginning of Your Relationship

One of the great rewards of a committed relationship is believing that you'll never have to go it alone when you're upset, unsure, or under pressure. Recall a time or situation when you felt the security of being part of that devoted team.

♥ EXERCISE: How Your Partner Responded to Your Need for Participation When Your Love Was New

In your journal, write about a time in the early months of your relationship when you were facing a problem and your partner was right by your side. Pick an important situation when you were grateful for your partner's compassion and participation.

Example

"We'd met three months before and had only been serious about our relationship for a couple of weeks. I'd told you I was running a marathon despite my bum leg but that I needed to stay in the race. My running buddy was laid up from his motorcycle accident and I'd promised I'd run the race for both of us. I knew it was a stupid thing to offer, but

I had to keep my word. I didn't tell you why, and you never pushed.

"You did ask if anyone was going to be there in case I had a problem. I think I said no, and that having someone there had never been important to me, because it never had been. I played every game as a kid without anyone there.

"I fell near the end of the race, and the pain in my leg was killing me. When I tried to get up, I felt support under my arm. I looked up and you were there. You had a knee brace with you that fit me, and some topical cream to help the pain. You just smiled and told me not to quit. When I crossed the finish line, you were gone, but your smile wasn't. I'll never forget that day."

Example

"I remember our first Christmas. I wanted so much to be with you that for the first time in my life I blew off going home. I didn't want to let you see my tears on Christmas morning when I missed being with family. Our lovemaking was phenomenal, and we had trouble letting go of each other. I knew that spending the holiday with you was the right decision, but I was still so sad inside.

"When we came downstairs, you insisted that I open up the big gift from you first. I couldn't imagine what you'd bought me that would take up that much room in my small apartment.

"After taking out all the stuffing you'd put there to fool me, I found a smaller box inside. It was a small laptop connected to a video calling service. You'd already sent one like it to my mom. I couldn't believe that anyone could care for me that much. I knew that morning that I never wanted to leave you."

When you've each written down your examples, sit across from each other and share them. Tell your partner first that you might be feeling strong emotions and you'd like to feel supported and understood. Tell your partner you don't expect him or her to feel exactly the same, only to listen as you describe how meaningful those times were to you.

♥

Suggestions

Whenever you compare the memories of beautiful times with less fulfilling ones in the present, you are bound to feel the grief of that difference. That is natural. Try to let those sad feelings go and concentrate instead on the touching memories you are now sharing.

You can bring back those memories without letting your current disappointment erase them. Remembering how much you once cared for each other will help you to recapture the sweetness of those wonderful memories.

Step Two: Evaluate Your Current Relationship

Depending on your scores from the Quick Check Meter test above, you and your partner might have a very different current experience of whether you act as a team or do things more separately. The comparisons between your early and current feelings may seem daunting, but whatever your memories are, try to face them courageously.

Hopefully neither of you left your team on purpose or with the intent to exile your partner into solo problem solving. Hold on to the hope and commitment that you can be best friends again someday. It will take work, but that goal is within your reach.

♥ EXERCISE: Why You Withhold Your Availability

The goal of this exercise is to help you understand the current situations that tempt you away from being a team. This exercise will help you recognize them and change them if you wish.

Write down a recent situation where your partner looked to you to be part of a team, and you sidestepped or refused the request. Use the following questions to help you remember the experience in detail. Write your example in your journal to create a narrative to share with your partner later.

1. What was the situation?

2. What did my partner ask for?

3. What was my immediate feeling?

4. How did I react?

5. How did my partner respond?

6. What did I do?

7. After I acted, how did I feel?

8. How was the relationship affected?

9. How do I feel now in retrospect?

10. Would I do it differently now?

11. If so, how?

Example

"It happened last week. You wanted me to come home from work because you were feeling lousy and the baby was sick. The night before, you had stayed up late with the neighbor watching movies while I was trying to get my business plan finished. I resented watching you have a good time while I had to work. I wanted to be more generous, but I couldn't seem to get there.

"It was after midnight when I asked you to come to bed. My shoulders ached from twelve hours on the computer and I needed you to care for me. You made some remark about my poor timing and promised you'd come in a while.

I think I fell asleep around one. You tried to get close but I pretended to be asleep. I didn't want you to know how much you had hurt me.

"When you called me that next day complaining about feeling sick, I told you I was too busy to talk. You blew up and said I was selfish. Me, selfish? That got to me. Hadn't you noticed that I'd pretty much stopped asking you for anything?

"When I came home, I wasn't nice. You kept telling me you were okay but I could see how sick you really were. I felt like a damned fool.

"In the past I would have gladly come home right away, put you to bed, and taken over. I'd have jumped in to help. I'd probably have cleaned the house and made you eat something nourishing. I feel terrible about this. I don't know how I got to be this way, but it's not okay anymore."

After you've written your own example in your journal, share it with your partner, and ask him or her to do the same. It is important that your partner not judge or argue. These are difficult scenarios to write, and even more difficult to share, but the more honest you can be, the more likely you will heal the rift between you. Embarrassment and humility can be the beginnings of self-forgiveness.

This exercise can be repeated as often as you find it helpful.

♥

Suggestions

This team-versus-solo disconnect affects everyone. Few partners in any relationship stay as automatically connected as they were when they were first in love. But committed lovers are open enough with each other to say when a need for participation is a 10 and when it is less important. Occasional slips are part of any relationship, but you must respond to crucial requests with willing and enthusiastic involvement.

Step Three: When Did You Begin to Drift?

You should not always expect that your partner will want to participate in all your decisions. Sometimes it is easier and more effective for both of you if personal issues are solved separately. But if your relationship ends up with too high a percentage of solo problem solving, you'll lose the team advantage you once had.

Partners may not understand why or even notice when their participation begins to diminish. But by the time they realize that their team connection is flawed, they may have become so used to handling challenges alone that reconnecting is harder than keeping the status quo.

Reasons for Going Solo

Intimate partners rarely intend to abandon their commitment to helping each other. When asked why they drifted from involved team members to parallel problem solvers, they usually aren't sure.

Sometimes the decline begins with one painfully separating incident. For instance, you may have refused to help your partner because you were still angry from a prior interaction when you were particularly sensitive to rejection. Your partner may have denied you in an uncaring way in the past that left you feeling hurt and abandoned.

At other times your partner may have wanted to be available but couldn't for reasons beyond his or her control. You may not have agreed that the justifications were reasonable, and you might have misinterpreted them as a rationalization for not caring. Once suspicious of motives, you became unwilling to forgive, adding that disappointment to a gunnysack of prior resentments.

An accumulation of smaller disappointments can lead any partner to stop asking for help or to reach outside the relationship instead. The negative spiral continues until there is no option but for both partners to operate in parallel, taking care of their own challenges as if they were alone.

♥ EXERCISE: When You First Remember Choosing Separateness Over Teamwork

Assume that you are a caring person who was once very sensitive to your partner's problems and eager to participate in helping. You didn't change that pattern intentionally or just to hurt your partner. You must have had legitimate reasons to abandon that commitment.

In your journal, write down a time when your partner needed you to participate in a solution and you declined. Then, after the entry, write your reasons and how they influenced your decision.

When you have come up with your example, ask yourself how you feel about the decision you made. Would you make it again today in a similar situation? What happened to your teamwork as a result of that decision? After you've answered, write your experience in a narrative and share it with your partner. Then ask your partner to do the same.

Example

"I remember the first time I felt this way. Though it was a long time ago, I've never really been able to let it go. Now that I'm recalling the feelings, I realize that I've been less participatory ever since.

"We were on our first vacation together, and I was really looking forward to our planning something new together each day, like a great team. But it didn't happen that way. We weren't a team. We were a totalitarian government with me as the only subject.

"From the moment you woke up, there was something I was supposed to take care of for you. You didn't remember your sunblock. You needed *real* coffee no matter how long the room service took to bring it. You needed me to hang up your clothes because you had to shave your legs and that way we could get going earlier. It didn't feel like a 'we' to me. 'We' to you was making sure that I got us on the right bus, selected the right tour guide, arranged the right agenda for the day. There was no point in arguing.

"I was so crazy about you that I would have done anything just to make you happy. Your multiple distresses just gave me more opportunities to help you, and I felt sure you'd be on my side when I needed you.

"It didn't happen. I should have known that there would always be more requests than I could ever handle, and you'd never forgive me for the ones I couldn't.

"I finally just told myself that it was okay to grant you every third request and still be a good guy. And I'd stop waiting for you to watch out for me. I just started handling my own needs. I guess I still do that.

"Now that I'm thinking about it, I'm not happy with this decision or my rationalization for it. It feels lame. I've pretty much written us off as a team and never given you a chance to change things with me. I think I've gotten a lot of mileage out of being a martyr and silently holding you accountable. I'm really sorry."

When you share some of these memories, your partner may feel upset, guilty, sad, or remorseful. But, interestingly enough, some others may bring a sense of relief and the hope that these memories, once shared, can be healed. You may both finally understand why you have allowed your team to disintegrate. Don't be discouraged. When you are willing to honestly share these important experiences with each other, you are creating a foundation for the kind of authenticity you will need to build your new team.

♥

Suggestions

You may not realize when you came up with your reasons to separate from your team or when you decided to redirect your energy. You have to break those patterns before healing can occur.

Step Four: What Stopped You from Healing the Situation at the Time?

Intimate partners do not always realize that their conscious or unconscious choices are creating an ever-growing emotional chasm between them. Wanting to ignore slights and stay connected, they purposefully overlook the disconnects that are happening between them, hoping they will not be that important in the long run. It may only be when a crisis or a series of blatantly negative experiences happens that they realize something is seriously wrong.

If you began as a loving team and now find yourselves often operating solo, you may have fallen prey to the same behaviors. From a place of consideration and compassion, you might not have wanted to burden each other with things you could handle on your own, and you may not have noticed the increasing frequency with which you solved problems separately. Once you got used to operating solo, perhaps you lost touch with the wonder of having someone to cover your back when times are tough.

To rebuild the beauty of the team you once were, you'll want to know why you stopped counting on each other and recognize the degree to which you are operating on your own now.

♥ EXERCISE: Why You Didn't Fight for Your Team

Write down an example of a recurring situation when you wanted your partner's participation and he or she didn't seem to want to make your partnership a priority. Tell your partner why you gave up trying to heal that rift, how the decision affected you then, and how it still does.

When you have finished, compose your own narrative to read to your partner later. The importance of this exercise is to help your partner understand how your past decisions have set the stage for how you interact with him or her now.

Example

"Damn, this exercise feels really uncomfortable. The minute I began thinking of what you did to avoid helping me through one of my most painful struggles, I realized we had stopped operating as a team. I know when I pulled away from you, and I'm still carrying the scars of that decision.

"You probably already know what I'm going to say, but I need to get it out if we're going to connect again.

"Before I was pregnant, we did everything together. I cooked, you did the dishes. I made our apartment beautiful for the parties, you always cleaned up. When we found out that we were going to have twins, you never missed a doctor appointment with me or a chance to read the stack of parenting books we bought. I almost felt like you were carrying the babies with me. It was the most incredible time of our lives and I knew we were in it together, like always.

"After they were born, everything changed. You were so crazy about your sons that I felt like a brood mare, sent off to pasture to heal myself while you drooled over your heirs to the throne. I cried myself to sleep at night when you'd roll over and ignore me. When I asked you to help me feel better, you just told me there was no problem and that I had nothing to be unhappy about. You handled your end of the deal, and you expected me to handle mine.

"I withdrew from you then, and I don't think I ever really came back. I acted as if it was okay to live parallel lives. We still had a few laughs from time to time, and the usual obligatory sex, but I always hid my heart. I guess I wanted you to push through my defenses to prove you loved me, that we were still the team we always were, but you didn't. Your career took off, and you were gone all the time. Whatever time you had at home, you spent with the boys.

"I've watched you reach out to me in your shy kind of way over the years since that happened, but I pretend not to notice. You never push me when I don't respond, and I haven't helped it get any better. My heart is breaking right now for all the loving times we've lost and for my not reaching out to tell you what I've been feeling for so long. I know it's both our faults, but now I understand that I'm the only one who can change me. I want to. I'm so sad that I stopped trying."

When you first tell each other these situations from the past, you may uncover unresolved emotions that you thought were taken care of. You also need to be ready to hear some thoughts and feelings that can make you feel sad, hurt, angry, or guilty.

It is crucial that you stay with the exercise and share those moments when you left your team, even if it is difficult. You will become more courageous with practice. Your goal is to face whatever decisions you made before that affect your relationship now. Finding even one crucial pattern will loosen your psyche's hold on others just under the surface.

♥

Suggestions

You can change established negative behavior patterns both by exploring their origins and by examining how those patterns still exist. The more deeply they are entrenched, the harder they may be to eliminate, but you are more likely to be successful if you bring them into focus. They are barriers that block the entrance to transformation.

Step Five: What Do You Need from Each Other to Become More Available Again?

Your relationship may feel a little like an emotional train wreck right now. These exercises are purposefully challenging, and your initial experiences may be daunting. However, these exercises are designed to bring sunshine into long-darkened places that once were beautiful. Those forgotten, sweet connections will come to light again when you start your process of healing.

♥ EXERCISE: Prioritizing Needs on Your Wish List

Make a list of things you need your partner to do to make you feel like you're on the same team again. Make certain that you share how important each need is so that your partner will be able to prioritize it accordingly.

Start with just a few entries the first time you do the exercise until you become skilled in this process. Your needs will understandably change as your relationship grows closer, and you will want to revisit this exercise on a regular basis.

Remember that you once were a winning pair, living in each other's hearts and willingly sharing your mutual resources. From that loving place, you could anticipate each other's desires and support each other's challenges. Your goal is to get to that place again.

After each entry on your list:

- Write down how long it has been since you felt confident to ask for this, and how you have felt without it. Include examples if they come to mind.

- Place a number from one to ten next to each entry to rate its importance to you. One is the least important; ten is the most.

- Describe to your partner how this change would help you to feel close again.

When you have finished, compose a narrative that includes all of your feelings and also rates the importance of your request.

This is not an exercise designed to punish either of you for the past. Hopefully it will give you more hope for a better relationship in the future. Encourage your partner by offering as many incentives as you can when you ask for a change of behavior. Also, use respectful humor when possible. It is a wonderful antidote to the fear of rejection.

Example

"I want us to spend more time alone together.

"I've missed the long, timeless moments when we'd find a special place and talk about all our fantasies. It was so spontaneous. We'd guess each other's thoughts and pledge our support of whatever the other wanted.

"In terms of importance, it's a 10.

"It would feel like we were back together again in the special way we used to be. I would feel grateful, happy, and more generous toward you again. Actually, I'd probably be ecstatic."

Example

"I need you to share my concerns about my crazy sister's alcohol binges. I know they have kept me away from you in terrible, unpredictable ways, but I feel so alone when I think about what could happen to her. You used to stay up and wait, or call me every hour to ask how I was, but now you just disconnect and tell me how resentful you are that I've been gone. I don't know what to do. I feel torn apart. I don't expect you to love her the way you once did, but I need you to support me because I still do.

"I need this when she's really gone off the edge and I'm afraid I'm going to lose her. If only you were in this with me again, I know I'd be less anxious.

"It's a 7.

"I would probably wonder if you really meant it, but be ever so grateful that you even tried. Now that I'm telling you, I can feel the sadness inside, and it's clear how much I've missed your support."

Example

"I want you to remember how important football is to me. When we were newly in love, we used to keep track of our favorite teams. Remember? We'd bring popcorn and cold beer and cuddle on the couch. We'd even try to scream in harmony and burst out laughing.

"Now you get up constantly to do other things. The way you halfheartedly act as if you want to be there feels so goddamn patronizing. I'm sorry for sounding angry right now. I know I'm supposed to be just asking for what I want. I guess it's still so important to me, and it seems so easy for you to forget something that's not important to you. I didn't realize I was stuffing my feelings about it.

"I thought this was a 7 but I guess it really is a 10. No, make that a 12.

"I'd feel great, but only if you enjoyed it as well. If only we could share that again. I'll even throw in some romantic evenings in gratitude. You get to set the itinerary."

♥

Suggestions

Be careful as you ask for these new team connections. It is tempting to bring up your partner's past failures in order to pressure him or her to do what you want. Instead, encourage your partner by trying to let go of past hurts, and put your energy into building these positive new behaviors instead.

Step Six: Rebuilding Your Team

Promises are only believable if they are kept. It is easy for all of us to get fired up about a new way of being together when we feel that our hoped-for needs will finally be addressed and our partner will be back on our side.

Keeping your partner's feelings in mind will help both of you to keep your promises. Some things will work better when you're a team, and some are okay to do alone. You and your partner must agree on which is which.

♥ EXERCISE: Working Out Your New Team Rules Together

Think of a situation that is likely to come up where one of you makes a request for team participation.

As the new team you want to be, your first step is to assess the situation together and decide how you can best combine your common resources to handle it.

Here are the three modes of cooperation you can choose among when planning together:

1. You'll work together to achieve the best outcome.

2. One of you can easily carry the task out alone and the other will stand by for reinforcement if needed.

3. You'll divide up what is needed and handle each part separately. Then you will reconvene to evaluate the outcome and make the next plan.

In asking for help, let your partner know what the situation is and how you want his or her participation. When your partner asks for your involvement, clarify what you need, and offer whatever you can to help you resolve the issue together.

Example

Requestor of team support:

"I'm dreading my mother's visit, and I need you to work with me when she's here. She continuously starts trouble between us by making up nonexistent problems. She'll put me down and complain about everything I do when I'm not there, and then try to get you to agree. You need to understand in advance that when you're kind to her, she will assume you are in agreement and tell me later that you are. Then she sits back and watches us fight. I don't want to hurt her, but I really need you to work with me on this."

Responder:

"I know exactly what you mean. It happens every time. I hate to be rude to her even though I know she's trying to stir things up between us, but I can see what you're up against. I'm not here during the day, but I can make sure I'm in the room when she talks to you at night. I think if she sees that we're not going to sell each other out, she'll get the picture. I can see you need all the help you can get, and I'm right here with you."

This situation is mode of cooperation number one. This couple recognizes they need each other's full participation to achieve the best outcome.

♥

Suggestions

Use as many examples as the two of you need to differentiate between the three modes of cooperation that partners make when they are a team. Whether you decide to work together, work separately with backup reinforcement, or divide up the tasks, talking through the process will help you feel that you are a team again.

Reflections

You might think that being willing to participate as a team would be guaranteed in any loving relationship. Unfortunately, it is one of the first behaviors to go if the partners feel unsupported. Once they lose their team perspective, they may begin to solve all their problems on their own and forget how important it is to share challenges and solutions in a committed relationship.

As undermining as this stumble may appear, it is one of the easiest to heal. Most partners who were once a loving team want to feel that way again. They remember what a joy it was to trust each other and to willingly participate in facing each other's concerns. When they learn where they lost each other and reaffirm their mutual support, they soon become a winning team again.

from **feeling unconditionally loved** to *being on trial*

"You loved me without question before. Now I have to fight to prove my worth."

If there is one consistent theme new lovers express, it is feeling totally accepted and treasured by their partners. They have found a safe haven in each other's presence: a place where every request is welcomed, love is bountiful, and forgiveness is guaranteed.

"When I'm in his arms, I'm home. We feel blessed to be together."

"The first time we were together, I felt I could tell her anything. She thinks I'm the greatest lover that ever lived. I'm unbelievably happy."

"No matter what I need, he's there."

"She's the first person I've ever told about my crummy childhood. I've never felt so supported. I wish I'd had someone like that when it was happening to me."

"He shows up at work and brings me my favorite dessert. No one has ever taken care of me like this before. I feel like I'm the most special person in the world."

"When she touches me, I don't know whether to laugh or cry. I've never felt this vulnerable before, or so safe."

Ecstasy. Joy. Sweetness. Excitement. Fulfillment. Hope. Security. Love. These are the words new lovers use to describe their experience. Wanting to maintain the exquisiteness of their love, they put aside any behaviors that could threaten the relationship and focus on whatever they can do to keep it alive. Because they are so committed to each other's safety and happiness, their unconditional support creates an upward spiral of spontaneous regeneration.

As the Relationship Matures

New lovers believe that their positive exchanges will go on forever. They pledge their resources to the relationship, willingly ignoring life's other priorities for as long as they can.

But, as the relationship develops, prior commitments and conflicting desires emerge, reclaiming the attention that has been directed toward each other. As the partners struggle to redistribute their resources, the intensity of their devotion to each other is also understandably diminishing. Though they are still just as committed to their relationship, they can no longer guarantee unconditional support.

Becoming More Realistic

As your love for your partner grew, you hopefully understood and accepted that your once-automatic availability to each other needed to be tempered by legitimately competing demands. You redefined which expectations were still high priorities and which were unreasonable or unlikely to be granted. Given that new understanding, you could still count on each other when your requests were crucial.

"I know she's on a deadline at work, but if I needed her, she'd be there. We do that for each other."

"He really looks forward to his nights out with his friends, but I know he'd be with me if I were in trouble."

"Even if she's got a lot on her plate, I know in her heart I'm still her first priority."

"He's always been there when I needed him."

New lovers know they have each other's unquestioned support. As their relationship grows, they are not always able to provide that automatic availability, but still must be able to count on each other in crucial times. If either partner is abandoned at an important time of need, he or she may no longer trust that a safe haven still exists.

If your partner no longer provides willing support when you are in trouble, your disappointment may drive you to behaviors that can be destructive to the relationship. If you find yourself pleading, coercing, manipulating, and threatening, you are in danger of pushing your partner farther away.

If you have been stripped of that once-guaranteed rapport, you may counter by withholding support from your partner during his or her legitimate emergencies. Now, as if on trial, both of you must negotiate for each moment of comfort and justify needs that were once guaranteed.

Please do not feel embarrassed if that's where you are now. It is all too human to act in counterproductive ways when fear of loss is the driver. Right now you are only exploring how far you have come from the safe harbors you once depended upon.

Has Your Relationship Lost Its Safe Harbors?

Were you once able to reach out to your partner any time you needed help, but now are reluctant to ask?

Do you feel you have to justify being cared for when you are hurting?

Does your partner seem reluctant to care for you when you're down?

Does it seem that you can only count on nurturing when you are in a significant crisis?

Can you count on your partner to put aside his or her own needs for you if you're in trouble?

Do you find it less painful to heal your own heartaches than suffer your partner's rejection?

These questions can be uncomfortable to consider. You may not have realized until now that you've stopped asking for comfort when you are in difficult situations. Perhaps you've had to go through so much distress to arouse your partner's support that you've stopped trying.

If you've drifted far from the safe havens you used to count on, that painful reality will eventually erode your intimacy in other areas. Experiencing rejection too often, you may now mistrust nurturing even when it is sincerely offered. To return to a happier state, you must re-create trust in each other's support.

♥ EXERCISE: Quick Check
Safe Haven Meter

The following statements will help you and your partner evaluate how far you have drifted from your safe havens.

Using the scoring system below, fill in each blank with the corresponding point number. After each score, write in your journal any pertinent feelings or thoughts that come to mind. These will be helpful when you and your partner share your responses.

My partner is always available = 1

I can count on my partner if he or she is in a good place = 2

My partner will be there for me if he or she thinks my request is valid = 3

My partner is only available if I promise not to ask for excessive support = 4

I can only get the nurturing I need if I am in a significant crisis = 5

My partner justifies his or her unavailability and makes me plead for attention = 6

My partner is unavailable = 7

1. When I'm hurting and need a safe place to be nurtured, _____ .

2. When we've been fighting and I need to feel close again, _____ .

3. When I've done something stupid and feel humiliated, _____ .

4. When I need caring but haven't been giving my partner what he or she needs, _____ .

5. If I feel overwhelmed and can't seem to find my way out of a mess, _____ .

6. If I know I should take care of myself, but I feel inadequate, _____.

7. When I'm down on myself and just need unconditional acceptance and love, _____.

8. When I need my partner to focus on me, even if he or she is preoccupied, _____.

9. If my requests seem superficial to my partner, but are important to me, _____.

10. If I need reassurance for whatever reason, _____.

11. If I've suffered loss or rejection outside the relationship and ask for support, _____.

Scoring

The higher your individual score, the more you may have lost confidence that your partner will be there for you if you need him or her. If your score is 20 or under, you still believe those safe havens are in readiness if you need to reach out for support. If your score is between 21 and 50, you may no longer have a safe place to rely on except when your partner agrees you are in a legitimate crisis. If your score is over 50, you have probably experienced significant mistrust barriers, and you'll need to begin your healing plan as soon as possible.

It may be more difficult to find that one of you feels safe when the other does not anymore. A twenty-point difference in your scores may signal that difference. Talking to each other about what a safe haven means to each of you may help you understand how your scores can be so far apart. Sometimes one partner needs more assurance that safety is available when needed. It is not wrong for there to be different desires as long as all are respected and accepted.

♥

The Healing Plan

Safe havens cannot be magically reconstructed or created on demand. They have likely been dismantled over time by multiple misunderstandings and unfortunate crucial moments when you withheld support from each other.

Your pathways back to trusting again may be obscured by layers of hurt or anger that must be understood and healed. You believed in each other's unquestioned support when your love was new. You may have lost that by inadequate communication or unintended unavailability.

Perhaps other priorities have emerged that neither of you anticipated. Maybe you unknowingly took advantage of each other at times and didn't realize you were doing so. It's possible that your partner did not know how to set boundaries and offered himself or herself in sacrifice. Or, what was sacred to you was not to your partner, and you face disappointments from those misunderstandings.

In any case, you have lost something sacred that both of you once treasured. Now you are on a virtual witness stand, forced to argue your case before being granted access to what once was your right.

The healing process for establishing new safe harbors should be gentle and deeply reverent. You must both develop a new and different kind of welcoming that is based upon the realities of your more mature relationship.

Step One: Go Back to the Beginning of Your Relationship

Though it can feel bittersweet to remember more fulfilling moments from the past, you'll be more successful in healing your present situation if you can. The lovers you once were are still somewhere inside of you. You haven't lost the knowledge or ability to love each other, but have perhaps forgotten what it was like or been worn down by frustrations.

New love is an ever-filling fountain. In those early experiences, couples are highly motivated to heal each other's every heartache and soothe every hurt. They hunger to feel safe in each other's arms, and to believe that comfort will always be guaranteed. They do not intend to deceive or make promises they cannot keep.

♥ EXERCISE: How Did Your Partner Once Provide a Safe Haven for You?

There were precious moments in your early relationship where you felt emotionally naked, opened your heart to your partner, and were welcomed and totally accepted. You may have been experiencing a crisis in your life, or perhaps something was happening between you and your partner that was worrying you. You reached out to your partner and found comfort, understanding, and support.

Whether you had known that feeling of total acceptance before or it was the first time, you knew you had found a place where everything would be okay.

In this exercise, reach back into those early memories and write several of those moments in your journal. Remember as many details as you can to help you reconstruct the experience. When you have those in mind, write narratives about them that you can share with your partner.

Example

"We'd only known each other a month, but already were spending every moment we could together. That day, we'd left each other after an incredible day together. We'd laughed so hard, I thought I would break in two. It was so hard to leave you each time we had to part.

"That night I was awakened by muffled voices outside my window. I looked at the clock and it was 3:00 a.m. I knew my doors were locked, and I was on the second floor, but I was still frightened.

"I'm so used to being independent and self-reliant, but I knew I might be in real trouble. I didn't want to bother you, but I didn't know what else to do, or who else to call.

"I'll never forget the strength in your voice. 'Honey, I'm going to call the cops, and then I'll be right there. Take your cell phone into the bathroom and lock the door. I've got a key. Don't even let the cops in until I'm there. Stay calm. I'll be there in ten minutes. Call me if anything happens. We'll take care of this.

"I felt immediately safe. I don't know if it was your tone of voice, or the way you effortlessly took charge. I just knew I'd be okay.

"You never chastised me for waking you or accused me of being too needy or overreactive. It did turn out to be two burglary suspects, and the squad cars picked them up, but I knew it wouldn't have mattered whatever it was. I never felt so safe in my life. On that night, you defined what love meant to me."

♥

Suggestions

Not all your important memories will be dramatic or crisis driven. They can be small things like your partner's remembering to bring you something that you needed for the Super Bowl party before you even realized you needed it. Or a time when your partner stayed up all night with you to keep you company just because you weren't feeling well. Or your lover's showing up with flowers the morning you started a new job or supporting you in a painful argument with a friend.

You can face anything with more courage when you know someone's behind you. The goal of this exercise is to begin the softening process that will bring back your trust in each other's support.

Step Two: Where Are Your Safe Harbors Today, and When Are They Absent?

When you and your partner compare the feelings you had when your love was new to the feelings you have now, you may feel sad about what you've lost. If so, please be kind to each other as you go through these exercises. Reexperiencing the beautiful memories of what once was will help you heal. Blaming each other, regretting what you've lost, or trying to erase the memories will only push you farther apart.

Though you may feel that your safe havens are gone, some still do exist, but it may just take more energy to access them. You must identify those that are no longer available as well as those that are still within your reach. You'll need that understanding to rebuild your legitimate havens again.

♥ EXERCISE: Comparing Existing Havens with Those That No Longer Exist

This exercise has three parts.

Part One: List in your journal at least five past experiences in your relationship where your requests for nurturing were welcomed and accepted. For each entry, you will create a narrative that includes the situation, your need, your partner's response, and your feelings afterward.

Part Two: List five experiences in the same period of time where your partner was unwilling or unable to grant your significant request. As with Part One, create a narrative that includes your needs, your partner's responses, and your feelings afterward.

Part Three: Compare the two lists. Can you find a pattern they share? Can you help each other to understand why each of you granted some requests and not others?

Example

"I had been working seven days a week for two months and I knew you were trying to be patient and totally support me. I remember the day you asked me if we could spend some meaningful time together. You weren't pressuring me or exaggerating your understandable frustration. I knew you were feeling lonely and unimportant, and I knew that I was neglecting you.

"I promised I'd find some time soon, but I never did. You were trying so hard to give me the space I needed, but I saw your unhappiness growing. I knew I owed you an apology and a real commitment, and I really planned to give you that as soon as I finished the project.

"Then my friends invited me to a once-in-a-lifetime helicopter skiing trip, all expenses paid. It was something I'd always wanted to do. I just couldn't pass it up, but I knew it would hurt you. I could already hear your words in my head, and you were right. 'You sure can find the time for what you want to do.' I didn't know how to approach you because I felt like a jerk.

"I'll never forget that morning I told you, fully expecting to get deservedly reamed. I laid out my conflicts and how guilty I felt. You were quiet for a long time. Then you said, 'You need this now, more than you need us. I can wait for when you want me as much as I want you. Please just make it soon, okay?'

"I remembered how kind you've been to me, so many times when I needed you in the past, and I realized how imbalanced I'd let it become. If I didn't thank you enough then, I want you to hear how much I appreciate you now."

Example

"I'm still hurting from this, but I'll try to say it as openly as I can. I don't ask you for much anymore because it seems that you do whatever you can to fix the problem just to get me off your back. I've worked on lessening my own needs so you won't feel that I'm too demanding, and I think I've done a pretty good job. But once in a while I still need you to be that person who wanted to be there for me when I needed you.

"The night I felt defeated, we'd seen the movie that had that violent rape scene. It brought back the pain of my own trauma. You were the first person I'd ever told what happened to me. You were unbelievably tender then, and every time since when the terrible memories surfaced, you would hold me until I stopped shaking. Because of you, they had quieted and I thought I was okay.

"After the movie, I couldn't stop crying. I felt like I was back at the time it happened to me. When I reached out to you, you seemed irritated and impatient. I remember pulling back, feeling stricken. Your response was, 'We've been through this so many times, babe. Just let it go. The woman in the movie wasn't you. What happened was a long time ago. Can't you put that behind you?'

"I felt like I'd been slapped. I know you were tired, and probably tired of my need, but I'm still crying inside. I didn't tell you then because I knew it wouldn't do any good, but I need to tell you now."

There is a difference in these two examples above. In the first scenario there was something new that could be understood and trusted in the present. The partner in need did not have to justify his desires or stand trial for his indiscretions.

In the second, it was an old heartbreak that never was fully resolved. Her partner did not understand the depth of her trauma or how important his support was. He did not intend to hurt her so deeply by his unavailability, but injured her by his untimely rejecting response.

In comparing your own examples, look for the differences in your two lists and the memories they bring up, then share those with your partner. Your partner should do the same.

♥

Suggestions

Of all of the stumbles, this one can cause the most grief in a relationship. The good news is that it also has the most capacity to bring love back. The unconditional acceptance you once experienced will never be as automatically available as it once was, but the more mature and practical emotional sanctuary you will create together will prevail despite life's challenges.

To better understand how you lost each other, you'll need to understand when your original welcoming began decreasing.

Step Three: When Did Your Safe Places Begin to Diminish?

Some couples maintain their mutual sanctuaries for months or years before they begin to diminish. Others are less fortunate. An unexpected challenge combined with a painful betrayal can temporarily or permanently destroy what was once sacred.

Though it may be disquieting to remember when and where you lost your trust in each other's support, those memories will help prevent you from repeating those patterns in the future. It is crucial that you hear each other now without arguing or becoming defensive.

When you tell your partner about the times when he or she has betrayed your trust, you are always risking being invalidated. It is difficult for anyone to hear information that creates embarrassment or guilt. Ask your partner to try to remain supportive. That skill will ensure that subsequent exercises are more successful.

♥ EXERCISE: When Did You First Notice That Your Safe Haven Was Becoming Conditional?

You may have difficulty piecing together the inconsistent experiences that made you aware your partner was less supportive than before. When those hurtful disappointments first occurred, you may not have seen them as important enough to challenge. Perhaps you rationalized them or doubted the legitimacy of your own needs.

In your journal, write about the first time you can remember reaching out to your partner with a significant need that was rejected or invalidated. Recall as many details as you can, using the following questions to guide you. If you feel comfortable, you can ask your partner to contribute information you may have forgotten.

When you feel the description is complete, create a narrative you will share with your partner.

Where were you at the time?

How long had you been together?

What was your request?

What happened when you asked it?

Were you surprised at your partner's response?

How did you feel and how did you respond?

How did it affect your willingness to make future requests?

Did it change the way you felt about your partner?

Example

"I do remember a time when I began doubting your caring and support. We were in Hawaii, scuba diving. I'd just been certified and was still pretty nervous. You seemed so caring at first, the way you'd always been. You couldn't have been more helpful and reassuring when I started to panic or thought I couldn't do it. I think we'd been together a couple of years, maybe three, but I know this was our first diving trip together.

"When I got stung by that jellyfish, I was terrified, and you were so concerned. Because you knew exactly what to do, I felt secure that I was going to be all right. When we got back to the hotel from the hospital, I was exhausted and still pretty traumatized. I was looking forward to spending the next few hours together settling down.

"We were sitting on the couch holding each other and I started talking about maybe watching a movie and ordering some take-out for dinner later. You looked distressed and were clearly uncomfortable. When I asked you what was wrong, you hesitated for a minute, then told me you really were looking forward to catching the last boat going out to get in one more dive that afternoon. You hoped I'd understand.

"I couldn't believe it, and I started to cry. 'Please, sweetheart, I'm still pretty shaken and need to be with you. Could you wait until tomorrow?'

"You looked at me with disdain, as if I were a weight around your neck. 'Don't overdramatize, okay? It's just a stupid jellyfish sting. You've got an antihistamine and a painkiller. What else do you need? You know how much I've been looking forward to this trip. I don't want to spend the rest of it babysitting you when you're perfectly okay on your own. Why are you trying to make me feel guilty?'

"I'd never seen you like that. I felt emotionally paralyzed and mumbled something about being sorry and wanting you to have fun. When you left, I knew I was crying over more than the sting. I felt as if I'd lost my best friend because I needed more than you thought I deserved.

"I know that you've been there many times for me since then, but I guess I've never really recovered. I never want to see that side of you again, so I've been careful not to depend on you anymore. I feel bad that I didn't tell you what was going on with me at the time, but I think I just tried to forget it. Now that I'm sharing it, I realize how abandoned and betrayed I really felt."

♥

Suggestions

If you and your partner have the courage and stability to do this exercise several times, it will help you understand where some of your fears have come from, and why you sometimes feel on trial with each other. The memories may be painful to dredge up, and even more difficult to share, but please try. Your ultimate goal is to know when and why those sanctuaries were destroyed and where they still exist.

Step Four: What Stopped You from Telling Your Partner at the Time?

When love is new, the partners in a relationship do express disappointment in each other's occasional unavailability, but they usually communicate it gently, confident that they will be reassured. Because they go out of their way to right any perceived wrongs, they also help their partners get better at doing what makes them happy. Focusing on their good connections and minimizing their distresses, they work to preserve the safe havens they both cherish.

As a relationship matures, the partners slowly come to realize they won't always be there for each other in the same way. Not wanting to confront that beautiful idealism, they may not even acknowledge the level of drifting that is happening. By the time their disappointments have mounted, it is harder for them to believe that a new, more realistic safe haven is possible.

If you and your partner have drifted away from the safe havens you once knew, please do not blame yourselves for waiting so long to share your feelings. It is hard to confront something that carries so much potential loss.

Because you had so many legitimate reasons to stay together, you may have just accepted the situation as inevitable and focused on what you could have instead of what was lost. This is a time to forgive each other for letting this crucial part of your relationship lapse, so that you can use your energy to rebuild.

♥ EXERCISE: Forgiveness

In your journal, refer back to the exercise in Step Three. Use the same examples you recalled when you went to your partner for support and did not get what you needed.

The goal of this exercise is to master the skill of authentic forgiveness. It is not about suppressing negative feelings or minimizing the legitimacy of your own needs. You're not interested in becoming a martyr or expressing unresolved feelings in other ways.

Authentic forgiveness has several components:

- You want to understand the bigger picture and keep your disappointments in perspective.

- You strive to live in your partner's experience as well as your own.

- You are committed to total honesty and what you need from your partner in the present in order to heal the past.

- You want to let go of any negative feelings that you have harbored and to love your partner freely again.

- You believe that working it out successfully will make it possible to expect a different interaction in the future.

Keeping those goals in mind, use the following statements after each entry to help you complete the forgiveness narrative you will share with your partner later:

1. Briefly describe the situation.

2. State what you needed from your partner and how he or she responded.

3. Try to put yourself in his or her place at the time and write what you think he or she was feeling. Do not assume there was a desire to hurt you.

4. What did you do?

5. Recall any times when you have not been there for your partner when he or she needed you.

6. Let go of any desire to blame.

7. Tell your partner what you still love about your relationship and what you need to believe in his or her love again.

8. Offer forgiveness for what happened.

Example

"After a humiliating fight with my boss, I impulsively walked out on my job. I cursed myself for my reactivity and my inability to handle him better, and obsessed over the situation for the entire hour it took me to get home. I knew you and I were on the edge and this was probably a stupid time for me to quit, but I just couldn't take it anymore.

"I desperately needed you to help me feel better about it, even though I knew I had put us in financial jeopardy and didn't have a right to your support.

"When I walked in the door, I smelled those special ribs I loved. You came to me looking beautiful and smiling in that heart-melting way that always gets me. I felt like an idiot, but I knew I had to tell you right away.

"I didn't know that it would hurt you that much. You dropped onto the couch and burst into tears. 'Oh my God,' you said. 'I splurged on dinner tonight because I thought I could spend the money. I feel ridiculous. What the hell are we going to do? Couldn't you have done something else, other than walking out? I'm so scared.'

"I felt terrible, like you didn't care about me anymore. I thought we were in this together and it didn't feel that way anymore. I felt so alone. I remember blowing up at you and leaving, slamming the door behind me. I drove around for an hour, hoping you'd feel bad about being so unsupportive.

"Now I realize I had never looked at it from your point of view. You'd been trying so hard to get me to stop spending and to be more responsible about money. I wasn't there for you, either.

"I don't want to blame either of us. I just want to concentrate on all the things I love about you. Even then, you were thinking about us. I know your heart and how hard you always try to help me. I want to erase what happened that night, honey, and to forgive you for how you responded. I also want to ask you to forgive me for all the times I probably let you hang when you needed me.

"Let's create a better way to be in the future. I can let go of any negative feelings from the past if I know we're back in this together."

♥

Suggestions

This exercise is the cornerstone of your healing together. Before you can build new, more mature safe havens for each other, you must clear the past of disappointments and misunderstandings.

Your future havens need to be based on more realistic expectations of each other's current availability. If you are honest and fair with each other, you'll be able to accurately predict when you can count on your partner's support. That way, resentments will not build and forgiveness will come more easily.

You should never have to give up the delicious entitlement of support that loving couples share in times of crisis, but you must negotiate those times with love and a strong sense of what is appropriate and available.

Step Five: How to Establish Your Mature Safe Harbor Together

Having understood when you lost faith in your automatic safe havens, and why you gave up trying to reestablish them, you're now ready to build more realistic expectations so that you can trust again in each other's availability.

Both of you must be able to rely on each other during times of crisis, but each of you may define a crisis differently. That different evaluation can cause misunderstandings if one partner feels he or she deserves something the other partner would not seek were the same experience happening reciprocally. One partner may also have more resources at any one time. It is crucial that both partners share their needs and expectations and not come to negative conclusions without checking the situation out first. To maintain the welcoming you need, you must commit to these sacred agreements.

Quality support means:

- Wanting to help your partner whenever you can, but not being automatically required to sacrifice for the other.

- Offering your partner emotional caring and validation even if you cannot satisfy his or her specific request at the time. It is crucial to not devalue a need simply because you cannot fulfill it.

- Not ever rejecting or embarrassing your partner for his or her needs, no matter what is being asked of you.

- Looking for other ways and times you can give without resentment, martyrdom, or inappropriate sacrifice and offering those gifts with generosity and enthusiasm.

The connecting truths are kindness and respect, no matter what request your partner makes. Welcoming gives both of you more hopeful options than uncaring rejection or withdrawal ever can.

♥ EXERCISE: Creating a New Safe Haven

There are several crucial points for you and also for your partner when creating your new safe harbor for each other. Go over these points together and then practice alternating playing each role. You can make up a situation just for practice, or use an actual situation from the past or one that is current.

If you need support at a crucial time, you should be ready to:

1. Approach your partner when you believe he or she can be available. You've learned when and how each of you is more likely to be receptive. This is the time to use that knowledge.

2. Share what you want clearly, telling your partner why it is important to you at this time.

3. Be ready to negotiate the balance between your need and your partner's availability, focusing on fairness, compassion, and absolute honesty.

4. Be able to take care of yourself if your partner can only give you part of what you ask for, and not punish him or her for what is denied.

5. In response, your partner should:

6. Respect your vulnerability and legitimacy when you ask for support.

7. Open his or her heart and be as available as possible.

8. Help you voice your request by supporting and understanding you.

9. Be honest and compassionate about what part of the request he or she can willingly grant.

10. Appreciate your willingness to be resilient if he or she is unable to help, and express gratitude for your forgiveness.

The example below incorporates the above crucial points.

Example

Your request:

"I've been waiting to talk to you about something that's really important to me. I know how stressed you've been, and I don't want to overload you, so I hope this is a good time.

"I desperately need to live in a place that feels more stimulating and alive. I've tried for a year to live in this remote place with you. It's really beautiful, and I know why you love it, but I'm so lonely and bored when you're not here. I know I agreed to do this for a couple of years and this may seem absolutely crazy, but I miss the chaos and craziness of the city. Is there any way we can rearrange our plans and move back? I'd never ask you if it weren't so important. I feel so bad about going back on my word, but I'm so unhappy.

"I'm willing to talk about what you need, too, and I want you to be okay with what we decide. If you need to think about it for a while, I understand, but please don't make me wait too long. I just need to know what I can count on."

Your partner's response:

"I'm really surprised, honey. I had no idea you felt so bad. I wish you'd told me sooner. I must be blind or something, but I'm glad you had the courage to tell me now. I want you to feel free to come to me, especially with something that's so important.

"I can see that you're embarrassed about not being able to keep your promise, and you might feel guilty about wanting me to give up the peace I need to complete this project. I know you came here with an open heart and tried your best.

"I'm pretty distressed to have to deal with this whole thing right now. It's a one-hundred-eighty degree change, and I need some time to think about it. But I promise that I'll figure something out, and I'll do it in the next couple of weeks.

"Please don't worry, but I'd appreciate your patience if you can just let me work this through. I don't want you to worry in the meantime, so if you need to take a couple of weeks and visit your mom in San Francisco, I'd really be okay. Whatever you want. What's important is that we can agree on a solution that will take care of us both the best way we can."

♥

Suggestions

When you practice this approach with your own examples, you will be more likely to feel receptive when your partner tries to understand what made you unhappy and tries to change his or her behavior. When anyone feels cared about, taken into consideration, and not obligated to respond the way you want, they often do.

Every couple has a history with complex layers of misunderstandings, disappointments, and loving experiences. The goal of this exercise is to create more safe harbors in your future.

Step Six: Protecting Your New Safe Havens

Whenever you have to resolve tender and vulnerable issues, you should make certain you have the privacy and uninterrupted time to adequately resolve them. Practicing the steps when your relationship is working well will give you the skills to act automatically when you are in crisis.

When you and your partner have created these new, reliable safe havens, you will be able to open up again, knowing your needs will be honored, your heartaches will be valued, and you will feel beloved even when things cannot be perfect.

♥ EXERCISE: Creating a Safe Harbor Sanctuary

This exercise needs to be done separately by you and your partner before you share your responses.

In your journals, describe in detail what a safe harbor environment would feel like to you. Be sure to let your partner know how your needs may change when you are in crisis and how you will let him or her know when that is happening. Think of the place you are describing as one where sacred rituals would be held, where all armoring, justifications, and fears are left behind. Describe this sanctuary and how you would be together there.

Example

"My perfect safe haven would be sitting with you at the beach in the evening. The ocean feels eternal and helps me keep my problems in perspective. We used to go there often when our love was new, and we always ended up closer. I need to be somewhere where there are no people and no distractions. I want us to feel timeless and not in a hurry. We could be wrapped in the same blanket, touching in some way, even if it is just holding hands. If we end up needing privacy, I want to go somewhere other than home, for just a little while."

Example

"My sacred place with you would be outside—a place that we would drive to together in silence, listening to music we both love so we could feel something good between us before we had to handle any rough stuff. I'd want us to spontaneously find a place to stop and eat a picnic lunch we'd packed together.

"When we started talking, I'd want us to be near each other, getting through the hard parts quickly so we could spend the rest of the time being close again. I'd hope we'd end up making love, but that's not a requirement. It just helps me feel that we're okay again."

♥

Suggestions

Your safe harbors may be emotional or physical. They will not always be the same for each of you, but they will share certain qualities. When you tell each other what you would like, look for ways to overlap your needs and your partner's, to create a sanctuary that can satisfy both your needs.

It's not always possible to go to your safe harbor physically when a crisis arises. But if you've gone there even occasionally, you can imagine being there when you need to. What is important is the atmosphere of welcome and nourishment you have created for each other.

Reflections

Of all of the stumbles, creating your new successful safe harbors together will be the cornerstone of your relationship and the most probable guarantor of your love's regeneration.

When your love was new, fulfilling each other's desires was uppermost in both your minds. As time went by, disappointments damaged and diminished the trust between you, and you no longer felt the same unconditional acceptance as you once did.

Now that you can understand how and why those misunderstandings occurred, you can create new safe havens you can both trust. Having that knowledge and commitment, you will find an acceptance and support that will hold when times are hard and flourish when they are good.

from **focusing on the relationship** to *pursuing outside interests*

"I know I'm gone a lot, but I need more stimulation."

When people first fall in love, they cannot get enough of each other. Immersed in the passion and intense focus that new love creates, the partners are captivated by the exquisite melding of their cultures, philosophies, values, and past experiences. As they affect each other in the present, they begin to create mutual dreams for the future.

"I could listen to him all day. I'm entranced even when he's just showing me how to change a tire. I'm fascinated by being exposed to things I've never known before."

"I've eaten tuna fish sandwiches my whole life. She adds these weird ingredients, and suddenly they taste like gourmet food. I never knew someone could be so creative with food. I'm unbelievably fascinated."

"I want to read every paper he ever wrote in college. Just knowing who he was then makes me feel proud. I want to climb inside of him and be part of everything he's ever done."

"She puts on a pair of skis, and it seems she's part of the mountain. I've seen pictures of when she had that skiing accident as a kid. To see her come back like this gives me so much respect for her."

"When my dad was killed, I wrote God off. Watching the beauty of her faith makes me want to try again."

As the Relationship Matures

As long as these delicious discoveries continue, you will keep looking to each other for regeneration, and you'll need little else. The mutual awakenings bring continuous new dimensions of intimacy, awareness, and seemingly limitless possibilities.

If you and your partner have been committed to a lifetime of personal transformation, you may be one of those rare couples that have maintained an ongoing sense of discovery. You may agree to pursue separate interests, but your primary relationship is always the highest priority for both of you.

Or, like most people, you may be better at pursuing a new relationship than keeping one alive. If you have fallen prey to that all-too-common pattern, you may have forgotten to continue growing as individuals, believing that the effortless interest of new passion would always regenerate on its own.

If you are always able to anticipate your partner's responses, and he or she does not offer any new or interesting experiences, you may have stopped looking to your relationship as your primary source of novelty and interest. Unless dramatic events reinvigorate your relationship, its magnetic attraction will give way to comfortable predictability. If so, you may go elsewhere to be reawakened and forget to bring that new energy back to your primary relationship.

How Couples Initially Cope with Dwindling Interest in the Relationship

If you are like most couples, you tried to increase your interest in each other when you recognized that you were drifting apart. Those emotional and physical bursts of reclaiming probably helped for a while, but without consistent energy, your relationship most likely returned to what it was before.

You're not alone. That result is so common that the bump-in-the-road sequence is frighteningly predictable. If your crisis-inspired efforts have failed to regenerate your interest in each other, the following pattern of drifting apart may feel all too familiar. As you examine the following stages together, share any reactions you may have with your partner and talk about how your experiences are similar and different.

Relationship Degeneration Stages

Stage 1. One or both of you attempts to arouse the other's interest by invitation, seduction, complaining, challenging, or dramatizing.

Stage 2. One or both of you attempts to get the other interested in outside new experiences you can pursue together.

Stage 3. You feel defeated and give up trying to regenerate interest between you, but you hope that pursuing your own outside interests will bring energy back into your relationship.

Stage 4. Feeling unable to maintain simultaneous connection pursuing new experiences, one or both of you choose to find that novelty without the other.

Stage 5. Having fewer new discoveries to share with each other, you try to focus on the positive qualities of your relationship to stay connected.

When you have shared where you are on this escalating sequence, you will hopefully be motivated to recognize these damaging consequences and recommit to pursuing discovery together.

Are Outside Experiences More Interesting Than Your Relationship?

- Do you find yourself sharing less about your outside activities with your partner?

- Have you given up asking your partner to participate in the activities you enjoy?

- Do you feel that your partner's thoughts and behaviors have become too predictable?

- Are you wondering if you can stay in the relationship the way it is?

- Do you still have the energy to keep trying?

As you read these questions, you may sense buried frustrations emerging. You might feel that you've already gone through all the stages above and couldn't get your partner to cooperate:

"I tried so hard to get her to work out at the gym with me. She knew when we married that I need to stay fit. I never wanted to leave her behind, but I can't give up my lifeline. Why can't she understand that?"

"He promises he'll take dancing classes with me, but he always has an excuse and I'm tired of going alone. There are plenty of other attractive men who would like to be my dance partner. I'm not going to wait much longer, but I'm scared that those experiences are going to become more satisfying than the ones we have together. Won't that eventually make me less willing to be close to him?"

You may be discouraged and wonder whether you can ever feel renewed in each other's company again. Yet you still care for your partner and wish that there was something you could do to bring back what you once had together, or to transform your current relationship into a newly intriguing one.

♥ EXERCISE: Quick Check
Relationship Focus Meter

The following statements are designed to help both of you evaluate where your relationship is now.

Using the scoring system below, fill in the blank with your corresponding point number. In your journal, write down any significant feelings or thoughts you may want to share with your partner later.

Most of the time = 6

More often than not = 5

Some of the time = 4

Once in a while = 3

Rarely = 2

Not anymore = 1

1. I'm happiest when I'm doing things with my partner. _____

2. My partner shares my interest in the things that matter most to me. _____

3. My partner seems eager and supportive of my outside activities. _____

4. I am interested in what my partner has to say and the things he or she likes to do. _____

5. I believe my partner misses me when we're apart. _____

6. My partner and I do new things together. _____

7. I see us as being willing to challenge our limits. _____

8. I believe my partner would still want to do new things with me if I asked. _____

9. I believe my partner really wants to improve our relationship. _____

10. Our experiences outside the relationship increase our interest in each other. _____

If your individual score is 40 or more, your relationship still has the magnetism to pull you back to each other. If it is between 21 and 39, your interest in each other is waning and needs regenerating. If your score is 20 or less, you need to begin closing that gap now.

The Healing Plan

Relationships have limited amounts of resources from which both partners must nourish themselves and their partnership. If they use those resources for their independent interests, they must bring back the equivalent or more when they return to each other for the relationship to maintain its potential for regeneration. Think of it as a delicious pot of soup. If partners only ladle the soup out and never put anything back in, it will no longer be able to nourish over time.

If your relationship is no longer your most important place of discovery and challenge, its life force will weaken. If that happens, your interest in each other will make outside involvements more desirable, taking energy from your primary relationship that it can hardly afford to lose. To renew that interest, you must recommit your energy to each other until your relationship is back on track.

In the following exercises, you will explore how and when your primary relationship lost its allure. Please be caring toward each other in this process. Remember, you once believed that you would be fascinated by each other forever. Like so many other well-meaning new couples, you didn't realize you could lose each other if you stopped transforming yourselves and your relationship.

As you work through the following steps, you will give yourselves the chance to again become the interesting partners you once were.

Step One: Go Back to the Beginning of Your Relationship

If you were like most other couples in the early stages of your relationship, you were intensely interested in what your partner's life was like before you were together. Childhood pictures, family stories, desires, fantasies, prior relationships, and dreams all seemed so incredibly important. You especially wanted to know why he or she chose you over all others.

The following exercises will help you recapture those early experiences. Please try to be open-minded when you revisit the nostalgia and sentimentality you felt then. It may be hard to face the extent to which you've drifted apart, but it's important that you commit to exploring these feelings. They will be instrumental in getting your relationship back on track.

♥ EXERCISE: Moments of Sweet Surprise

Recall several examples from early in your relationship where you found out something about your lover that affected you deeply, and write them in your journal. Along with each entry, describe the situation, what you discovered, and what made you want to know this person more deeply.

Example

"I remember the first time you invited me to have dinner with your parents. You told me that it might be uncomfortable, but that you needed me to know your family before I made a commitment to you. I was touched by your willingness to let me in, despite your obvious discomfort.

"When we got there, your dad was pretty drunk. I saw your expression change and watched your body tighten. I tried to help by being friendly and kind to him, but when he started flirting with me, I silently signaled you for help.

"I saw you take a deep breath and walk over to face him. You told him in a quiet but firm voice that his behavior was inappropriate. His started mocking you and took a step forward as if to start a fight.

"You didn't move, but your voice had a firmness to it I had not heard before. 'Dad, that's enough. You're acting like an ass. Go to bed.' Your father stood there for what seemed like an eternity, his facial expression shifting between rage and childlike terror. Then he turned and left the room.

"When your mom tried to offer a tearful apology, you took her in your arms to soothe her. I could tell it wasn't the first time, and I cried inside for you and for her. I didn't move or speak until she seemed all right. Then I asked gently if there was anything I could do. You looked at me with such tenderness and appreciation. I reached out and hugged your mom, feeling her broken heart. I told her everything would be okay.

"We drove to my apartment in silence and you dropped me off, telling me you'd be back in the morning after you checked on your mom. Home alone, I cried for all the times when I was young and in trouble and no one ever comforted me. I knew then that I wanted to be with you forever."

♥

Suggestions

The goal of this exercise is to recall the moments in your early relationship when you were deeply moved by your partner. When you share them, you may find that your partner was completely unaware that he or she had such an impact on you or doesn't remember the details the way you do. It doesn't matter. Your goal is to remember how sweet it was to be spontaneously fascinated by someone you adore.

Step Two: Being Together or Being Apart

This step will reveal the ways you have drifted apart and highlight the areas where you still look forward to being together. You'll also be identifying the outside interests that have taken precious resources from your relationship.

♥ EXERCISE: What You Still Enjoy Together and What You Enjoy More Apart

In your journal, write two separate narratives. Both will deal with experiences, ideas, or relationships that spontaneously interest you.

In the first, write as many as five things that you still enjoy with your partner. In the second, write as many as five things that you enjoy separately.

Choose examples that are significant and are accompanied by strong feelings. The more these examples mean to you, the more they will mean to your partner as you begin your healing process.

First Narrative

Example

"I still love seeing you at the end of the day. Your car pulls into the driveway and I feel complete, like everything is the way it's supposed to be. Maybe it's the way you smile when you see me, as though you wouldn't want to be anywhere else. I'll always treasure evenings in my life because of what you mean to me."

Example

"You have this wonderful way of messing up words that makes us both laugh. You don't seem to mind when I tease you about it. You've always been a great sport. I just realized it, honey. I'm sure other people don't have that kind of resilience. I appreciate you so much."

Second Narrative

Example

"I need to be with people who are excited about what's going on in the world. I hurt for people suffering tragedies in their lives. You always put me down because you think it's really stupid for me to worry about something I can't do anything about. Then I feel separate and alone. When I join causes, I'm with people who sympathize and are like me. It makes me feel like I'm not the only one who cares."

Example

"We spent so much time having great times together when we were first together. We hiked in beautiful places, went on exciting adventures, met new people, and got involved in so many things. We were a great team, remember? We used to be like twin magnets, attracting anyone we wanted to join us because of our great energy.

"Now all you do is work and then come home and sit. You're either on your computer or watching TV. You're too tired to talk and never interested anymore in what I've done while we've been apart. I miss the person I conquered the world with. I have to feel alive, and I can't let myself die inside. I've found friends who love me that way. I'm so sad you don't seem to enjoy me that way anymore."

♥

Suggestions

Telling your partner that you have lost interest in your relationship is very difficult. He or she may feel defensive when you speak of your disappointments or may want to blame you for checking out. You may find that your partner is unaware that you are not as focused on the relationship as you once were.

In order to begin healing the distance between you, please be willing to look at your own contributions as well as your partner's. It will take both of you working together to bring that spontaneous curiosity back.

Step Three: When Did You Begin to Shift Your Focus?

The process of drifting may have been so subtle that your day-to-day disappointments were easily overshadowed by your positive interactions. People who love each other are likely to suppress their disappointments and exaggerate their satisfactions. Unfortunately those unexpressed sorrows can create underlying disconnects that may not be noticeable until they have become entrenched.

An unexpected crisis can create a temporary reconnection that can give the illusion that your intimacy is still intact. But when the crisis is resolved and the requirement for energy, focus, and cooperation decreases, your intimacy level will return to where it was.

Many partners, somehow knowing that their interest in each other has been diminishing, often unconsciously or consciously create situations that are exciting to reinvigorate their relationship. Can you recall a time when you spontaneously decided to get a puppy, move into a new neighborhood, change jobs, or impulsively sign up for an exotic vacation? Perhaps, at some level, you understood that the novelty created by those extemporaneous decisions would, at least temporarily, regenerate your interest in each other.

In the following exercise, try to remember times when your focus began to shift away from the relationship and you knowingly pursued outside interests rather than trying to reconnect with your partner. You'll want to remember if you felt guilt, sorrow, rebellion, or even self-righteousness when you shifted your devotion.

♥ EXERCISE: When I Remember Giving Up Hope

In your journal, write as many as five memories of times when you gave up trying to get your partner to help you regenerate a sense of discovery in your relationship. In your narrative, write what you decided to do instead and how you felt about taking your energy elsewhere.

Example

"I remember the night in San Francisco when I wanted to be with you and you turned me away. I woke you up in the early morning because I hadn't been able to sleep and I couldn't hold my feelings in anymore. I told you then about my desires and disappointments in our love life and how much I wanted us to rediscover the closeness we had lost. Instead of listening, you were irritated and defensive. You kept telling me that I was making too much of it, and that everything was fine. You even chastised me for being self-centered and not understanding how men show love differently from women. Overwhelmed by your inability to love me that morning, I pulled in and didn't talk about it again, but I somehow hoped that you did hear me and just couldn't admit it.

"I remember the night I finally gave up hope. It was New Year's Eve, four years ago. We made our resolutions together under that old piece of mistletoe and the kiss was great, like it used to be. You looked into my eyes and told me things would be different from now on.

"When we got home from the party, you were so drunk that you passed out. I remember sitting on the side of the bed, crying out to an unconscious person and wondering why I had tried so hard for so long.

"I called a taxi and went back to the party. It felt terrible to be there without you, but I couldn't give up my life for you anymore. I got home at four o'clock in the morning and you were still asleep. I felt such a combination of guilt and self-righteousness, but I somehow felt that I still had some value. I know this isn't the answer, but I don't know what else to do."

♥

Suggestions

These moments may be painful to recall, but I hope they will motivate you to put your energy into healing the breach between you. Looking back, there may have been other options, but you couldn't see them because of your heavy feelings of exhausted resignation. Now is the time to look back at why you chose to find your interests outside the relationship.

Step Four: What Stopped You from Staying Focused on Your Relationship?

Being accountable for your own behavior is the only pathway to transformation, but please do not add self-blame to that process. Judging yourself negatively will stop you from growing beyond your past limitations.

♥ EXERCISE: Have My Behavior Patterns Kept Me from Staying Connected in Past Relationships?

To understand what you might have done differently, you'll want to identify your similar response patterns in prior relationships. Go back as early in your life as you can remember to understand where those responses first happened.

Use the following sequence as your guide.

- You felt that you were intrigued and fascinated within an important relationship.

- Your interest, or the other person's, began to lag.

- You tried your best to do whatever you could to reinvigorate the relationship.

- You were unable to get the other person to change.

- Though losing hope, you didn't want to give up.

- You looked outside the relationship for something that you could bring back to create new interest.

- Your efforts did not change the situation.

- Your motivation to save the relationship diminished and you continued to go outside the relationship for your own regeneration.

- You found yourself grieving the loss of connection with your partner but felt resigned because you were unable to get him or her to respond differently.

In your journal, recall three significant prior intimate relationships where you disconnected, then write a narrative you will share with your partner later. Use the following statements to guide you.

- Describe the relationship in enough detail for you to remember why it was important and what happened.

- Recall when you began to feel your interest diminishing.

- How early in the relationship did you begin to disconnect?

- How did you try to repair it?

- Describe the other person's response.

- What outside interests did you pursue?

- What happened to the relationship as a result?

- If you could go back in time, what, if anything, would you do differently now?

Example

"I'm thinking of something that happened between me and my best friend, Emily, when we were in the eighth grade. I feel tears coming now, just from bringing this memory back. We were so incredibly close, sharing every worry and every dream. We lived in each other's clothes and ate off the same plate. We lusted after the same boys, loved and hated each other's parents, pooled our money, and planned a future where we would never be without each other.

"As if it were yesterday, I remember when I began to break away. My family planned a trip to Europe the summer I turned fifteen. I was so thrilled to be able to do some of the things Emily and I had always dreamt of. When my parents offered to take her, it seemed as if my life had been touched by a rainbow.

"I literally ran the seven blocks to her house to tell her, expecting her enthusiasm to match mine. Instead, she became quiet and began to cry. Then she told me that she was too afraid to leave her mom and to travel that far away. I was stunned. Were all our plans only fantasies in her mind? I tried everything I could to convince her to change her mind, but she would not.

"When I returned from Europe, Emily was there waiting for me, eager to hear about my trip. I tried to be civil and act interested, but I knew that things would never be the same between us. I wish I had talked with her about how I felt, but I just kind of drifted and never told her why. I think I convinced myself that I did more to keep our relationship intact, but I really didn't. I feel so guilty now, being so self-centered. I think I will always miss her.

"As I'm reliving this, I realize that I still split off when I feel a relationship can't go beyond its limitations and is facing an inevitable end. I'm sure I do try to save it at first, then just give up without giving the other person a real chance. I've probably just been giving in to my own limitations blaming it on the other person. I want to change that."

♥

Suggestions

Like many people, you may find it difficult to handle the emerging feelings of sadness or regret brought on by doing this exercise. It's so much easier to blame the other person or the situation rather than looking back at your own responses, but if you can stay with the lessons that are yours, you will empower yourself to change your current relationship in a new way.

Remember, engaging in new interests outside a relationship is only a problem if it takes important resources from the relationship without replenishing them.

Step Five: What Do You Need Now to Refocus on Your Relationship?

If you are now involved in satisfying outside interests, you may be understandably resistant about giving them up. It is important to identify those interests that have drained resources from your primary relationship and those that have helped you regenerate your interest in your partner.

In the following two exercises, you will discover which of your outside interests have diminished your interest in each other and which have actually enhanced it.

♥ EXERCISE: Evaluating Outside Interests

In your journal, make two lists. The first will be the outside experiences that have taken time and energy away from your relationship.

The second list will show those that have replenished the relationship even though you pursued them separately.

Using your entries, write a narrative for each experience that includes any details or emotions that will help your partner better understand what has pulled you away.

List One: Outside involvements that took crucial resources away from my primary relationship

Example

"I'm studying with my new friends until late in the evenings a couple of nights a week. We share wine and stories and don't mention any other personal involvements.

"I like who I am there. I feel wonderfully independent. They know me as just me and not as part of a couple. They laugh at my jokes and ask questions about what is important to me. When I come home, I don't feel like sharing because I don't want you to put down my fun by acting competitive."

Example

"I go to the gym by myself now. I know I'm really addicted to working out, but I feel healthy and younger when I do. I'm noticing how much better shape I'm in, and it makes you less attractive to me. I'm also starting to notice other guys more, and it seems reciprocal. I used to bug you about this all the time because it's so important to me and I was afraid that we'd end up breaking up if you didn't do something about it. Now I'm more worried because I'm not seeming to care as much about whether you change or not. I think it means I'm starting to pull away."

List Two: Outside involvements that bring me back excited to share my life with you

Example

"At the free clinic, I see so much tragedy: so many people with nowhere to go and no one to care about them. I think about us a lot when I'm there. I'm grateful that you still love me and care so much about our relationship. I always look forward to coming home and sharing the meaningful things that happen there. You're always so interested in what is important to me."

Example

"In my martial arts class, my sensei's demand for discipline inspires me to be a better man. I want to be that guy with you because I know you'd feel more loved if I were. I appreciate the way you encourage me to be so involved with this without complaining about how much I'm gone. I think I'm going to push you a little harder to make it part of your life, too. I'd love this to be a way of life that brings us closer. It would double my pleasure."

♥ EXERCISE: What I Want from You, and What I Can Give You in Return

Again, in your journal, make two lists. First, write five ways your partner could help you restore your interest in him or her. Second, write five things you could do to restore his or her interest in you. When you have finished, write your ideas in narratives to share with each other.

List One

Example

"I would love it if you would turn off the TV so we could spend more time learning new things together. I don't mind watching TV once in a while, but how about going to that funky movie house near the university and seeing some student films? We could go out for coffee afterward and pretend we were the characters, the way we used to when we were first in love."

List Two

Example

"I know you once loved to look at all of those architectural magazines and dream about designing our own home someday. When it became apparent that we would never be able to afford the things you wanted, I didn't want to keep dreaming about something that would never happen and didn't want to talk about it anymore. I know I hurt you. Your fantasies were probably symbolic of other things that had meaning to you and helped you cope with other real disappointments in your life. I need to be more available to take part in any of your dreams, even if they aren't likely to come true. I'm so sorry for being such a downer."

♥

Suggestions

This is the most important step in creating a relationship that will hold your interest and inspire you to know each other again. As you can see, it requires a redirection of energy and a renewed commitment. It also requires that both of you continue to grow in new and unpredictable ways.

Outside interests can offer novelty and new possibilities that same-old relationships cannot. If you feel that you have stopped transforming, you will become predictable and less interesting.

Step Six: Keeping Your Relationship Your Primary Focus

Consider the effects of your separate interests on your relationship. Positive outside activities will enhance your primary relationship and keep you interested in each other. Negative ones will weaken your relationship and encourage you to continue to seek stimulation elsewhere. Couples who want to stay together talk about the effects of their separate activities and choose those that bring them closer.

The actual amount of time partners spend away from each other is also important. Unless your relationship is easily enriched and holds steady without needing a lot of time together to keep it thriving, you will always need to allocate enough prime time for each other before you take that resource elsewhere.

♥ EXERCISE: Planning Your Time Together

In your journal, write down the times during the day or night when you have the most energy and desire to connect with your partner. Make separate entries for work days and days off.

Pick one activity that would help you stay connected, and note the best time to participate in it. Ask if your partner would do that one thing for you this week if you reciprocate the following week. If either of you has to give up a separate activity to do it, you can negotiate a compromise. Try to pick experiences that feel right to both of you, even if one of you temporarily benefits more.

After you've completed the activity, you and your partner should openly discuss whether what you did brought you closer together and decide whether doing it again will increase your success. It doesn't have to be perfect. Partial successes can lead to more satisfying future ones.

Example

"My best time of the week is Saturday afternoon, when I've had a chance to get some sleep and the major errands are out of the way. At about three o'clock, I always feel adventurous and wish we could do something together. I know that's your basketball time with your friends, but I'd be so grateful if you guys could get together at another time.

"I imagine doing something outside first, like a hike somewhere beautiful, then shopping for stuff to cook together. I'd love to have our favorite music playing and take time out to dance if we felt like it. No phone calls, unless it's a real emergency, and we have to agree.

"I picture sitting in the Jacuzzi as the stars come out. I'd even love it if it were raining. I'd like to talk then about our dreams, pretend they could come true, and imagine how we'd feel if they did. Then we'd make love if we both wanted to.

"I know I haven't asked for this much in a long time, and I usually just disappear and pretend to be busier than you are. I get so discouraged when it seems like you'd much rather do something else than be with me. It's scary to open up, but I want to spend more time with you again."

♥

Suggestions

This exercise may seem simpler than it actually is. Having spent so much prime time away from each other, you may feel a little reluctant to open your hearts to more connection again. It is natural to feel that way because of the losses of the past. This is the time to take that risk. You once believed so deeply in your ability to generate joy together. You can again.

Please remember that things weren't this way when you were first in love. You'll never be intertwined in the same fused way as before, but you can once again be each other's most important person.

Continue to alternate your desires and experiences each week until both of you feel that your priorities are back in order. After a while, those positive connections will happen spontaneously. Stay in touch with each other if you begin to feel excluded, and recommit before you drift too far apart again.

Reflections

You may have had many legitimate reasons for shifting your interest away from your primary partner. Perhaps you felt disappointed or rejected once too often. Maybe your old relationship patterns have taught you to quit too early or stay until you are driven to run. Your relationship could be suffering from poor time management or competing priorities that have siphoned its resources.

Somewhere along the way, you stopped trying as hard, and you began to look for satisfaction and discovery elsewhere. You may have sincerely invited your partner to share those new dimensions with you, but were unable to influence him or her. Or maybe you wanted your partner to be the one who pursued intimacy and could not make that happen. As a result, your life's compartments have become more exclusive.

Now is the time to recommit to what you once had and could have again. It will take both of you to succeed. Transforming as a couple together is one of the most challenging and satisfying parts of any long-term partnership.

from **common goals**
to *different dreams*

*"We just don't want the
same things anymore."*

New love's magnetic attraction is undeniable. Two minds are melded into one, two hearts beat to the same rhythm, and musky, wonderful lust pervades. If those life-enhancing experiences are what jump-start a relationship, a couple's commitment to the same goals and dreams keeps it together. Sharing beliefs, values, and goals, they see themselves as united, striving for the same things in life.

"I couldn't believe how often we agreed on what was important, even down to the places we want to travel and the kind of weather we both love."

"He finishes my sentences for me. I am constantly amazed that he can always guess which restaurant I'll want to go to, and even exactly what I'll order. And I can do the same for him."

"I was concerned that she wouldn't understand, but when I told her my feelings about God, she completely agreed. We're both kind of searching in the same way. I felt so incredibly supported and validated."

"He came from a traditional household, just like I did. We don't want to be like that. We want to be equals in our relationship, sharing everything we do. I could never be with someone like my dad."

"We cry at the same parts in movies. It's unbelievable. I've never felt so close to anyone."

Aspiring to the same emotional, physical, and spiritual dreams and goals, the partners bask in the comfort of knowing they want the same things in life. Those common beliefs form the most reliable trust a couple can have.

As the Relationship Matures

As they spend more time together, the partners may find that the goals and dreams they shared at the beginning of their relationship often change over time. Unforeseen challenges and unexpected traumas can uproot any prior commitment, no matter how well-intentioned. A couple's capability for flexibility and adaptive skills may not be tested until they realize that they may no longer be on the same page.

New Challenges

Partners who experience their goals and dreams diverging are understandably threatened. One or both may feel betrayed and may try to invalidate the other partner's new choices or pressure the other partner to recommit to his or her original promise.

If that wayward partner is determined to go in a new direction, these attempts usually fail and can sometimes have the opposite effect. They can make that partner feel trapped or even pushed farther away.

Please do not feel your relationship has failed if your once-cherished mutual aspirations have lost their initial allure. You may have to find new goals and dreams that incorporate both of your needs, while maintaining respect for what you originally built together. That takes patience, openness to new directions, and the unwavering commitment to try every possible option to stay united.

Is Your Relationship Suffering from Diverging Goals and Dreams?

- Have you begun to wonder if your own dreams and goals are still the same as your partner's?

- Does your partner say things that make you doubt his or her commitment to what you both once believed?

- Do you feel the loss of your partner's support in crucial areas you once both embraced?

- Does your partner seem to be considering goals that are no longer familiar or desirable to you?

The sacred place you built when your love was new protected your relationship by keeping you committed to the ethics and behaviors that brought you together.

But you may have formed that bond prematurely. Caught up in new love's magnetic field, you may have minimized or suppressed any desires you had that did not seem to fit in your relationship. Now, they may have reemerged, and you no longer want to live without their being a part of your future.

♥ EXERCISE: Quick Check of Your Openness to New Common Goals and Dreams

The following statements will help each of you evaluate the level of support you have for your partner's right to create new ideals and goals. To score, fill in the blank with your corresponding point number. As you examine each question, write any significant feelings or thoughts that may come to mind.

Support him or her completely = 1

Am willing to look at new possibilities = 2

Feel skeptical but still open = 3

Feel resistant to what is being asked = 4

Feel somewhat threatened = 5

Am unable to accept the situation = 6

1. When my partner talks to me about new ideas and experiences to explore, I usually _____.

2. If my partner questions traditions that we have always practiced, I _____.

3. When my partner tells me that our original goals don't work for him or her anymore, I _____.

4. If my partner tells me that I am too attached to the past, I _____.

5. If I see my partner as less interested in our established ways, I _____.

6. When my partner suggests something unfamiliar, I _____.

7. If my partner feels I should be more open to new possibilities for us, I _____.

8. When my partner wants us to be freer in what we pursue, I _____.

9.   If my partner tells me that our relationship will no longer work unless we change the goals we once had, I _____ .

Scoring

If your individual score, or your partner's, is 18 or less, you have either maintained your initial agreements or successfully renegotiated changes and still feel connected in the things you are striving toward.

If your score is between 19 and 36, you are not allowing new goals to form that will keep you from drifting apart.

If your score is over 36, your desires and dreams may have become more divergent than you were able to recognize. If so, you need to work hard now to create new dreams you can both embrace.

♥

The Healing Plan

The six steps of your healing plan will help you commit to a new set of goals and dreams that will represent both partners' current desires.

As you execute these healing steps, you may feel emotions you were not aware of before. You may have abandoned goals that are still important to your partner. Or perhaps you want to pursue new ones that he or she would not choose to explore.

For example, many partners want to change their sexual patterns but fear their partners would be offended or uninterested if they asked. Some people who were once deeply religious either soften their long-held views of God or want to switch to a totally different spiritual path. Some couples made an early mutual decision that they wanted a large family, but now one feels that two children are enough.

You may even find that you have known all along that you wanted some things that your partner did not, but you didn't share your feelings for fear of threatening your relationship. Or you may each no longer feel the same way as you did in the beginning, but have pretended to feel the same so as not to cause disappointment.

On the other hand, you may find that being open about how you really feel will reveal a much closer match than you thought. Instead of feeling sadness for what you have lost, you could feel exultation for what is now possible.

The six healing steps will help you:

- Recall your original agreements

- Recognize when you and your partner began to diverge

- Create a new set of mutual dreams

- Plan for how you will keep them alive

Step One: Go Back to the Beginning of Your Relationship

Most couples in Western society have the freedom to select partners from diverse cultures, ethnic origins, political persuasions, and past histories. The multitude of options that freedom creates is both exciting and confusing. Common goals and dreams can be an interwoven blend of those multifaceted backgrounds or a conglomeration of misunderstandings and mistakes.

In the lust, excitement, and confidence of new love, most new partners don't consider that their common ideals and goals would ever diverge. They don't think about the personal goals they left behind or how their commitments might change when those goals reemerge.

To understand where you are now and what you have left behind, you must reexamine the aspirations you chose to give up in order to commit to your partner. Some may no longer be as important as they once were, but others will have grown in intensity because they were suppressed.

♥ EXERCISE: Your Goals Before You Were in This Relationship

This exercise will be in two parts. The first will be the memories you have of the goals and dreams you had before you knew your current partner. The second will be what goals you chose after you and your partner were together. You'll want to identify those you left behind to make your relationship work.

Write in your journal any significant feelings or thoughts that come up when you recall the memories in each part of the exercise. The narrative you create will be important to share with your partner later.

Example

The goals I had before I met my partner:

"Since I was a teenager, I've known what I wanted out of a relationship. My fantasy partner and I would finish college and graduate school while living together, marry by age twenty-eight or so, travel the world together, and then mutually decide to have three children within five years.

"We'd live in a rural area, have a beautiful garden, hold intimate soirees with great friends on the weekends, and share wonderful conversations and great wines late into the night. We wouldn't embrace any established religion, but we would constantly remind each other how blessed we were, and how willing we would be to help each other pursue anything that was important to either of us. We'd save a little money, but mostly focus on the joy of the moment, and never be limited in ideas or possibilities.

"I see how idealistic that seems, but it still feels like a great life to me, and I'm going to do everything I can to make it go that way."

Example

How my new goals emerged:

"My fantasy didn't develop the way I'd planned. I finished graduate school at twenty-five and didn't find the love of my life until I was almost thirty. By that time, I'd traveled quite a bit on my own, and my wanderlust had significantly diminished. I always thought I'd find my dream girl in some serendipitous moment on an unplanned adventure, but I fell desperately in love with you on a subway train in New York.

"When you shared your love of God and your determination to be a missionary, some part of me knew I should probably say good-bye. You were determined to change the world whether you had a partner or not. I didn't share that burning desire. In fact, it seemed about as far away from my goals as I could have ever imagined.

"But I couldn't stop looking at that beautiful light in your eyes. I knew that you had to do what you believed you came into this world to do, and if I was going to be with you, our mutual goals had to include your dream.

"We realized very quickly that we wanted to spend our lives together and would need to work hard on making some pretty tough compromises. You agreed to one child if we would first live in a third world country for five years. When we returned, we'd have a baby and I'd stay home to write the novel I always dreamt about while taking care of our child and you would get a job to pay the bills until I sold my book.

"Because your spiritual beliefs were so important to you, I agreed to sincerely explore the possibility of conversion some day. I loved you so much, I think I would have become a priest if you'd asked me to. I never felt resentful or martyred in the choices we made together, and I know you didn't either. We knew we were a great team and nothing could stop us."

♥

Suggestions

If you open your hearts, this exercise will bring up poignant memories. When you share these with your partner, you may find that, knowing what you know now about life and each other, you might not make those same commitments now.

Do this exercise without expressing any resentment or remorse. You chose your path together from your heart for the right reasons at the time. Whether you would choose them again now does not invalidate their rightness then. Do not blame each other for the innocence that new love provides.

Step Two: Which Common Ideals and Goals Still Exist, and Which Have Changed?

It can be difficult to examine the difference between the personal goals each of you had before you met and what you left behind when you chose to pursue mutual dreams. In your eagerness to blend together when you were first in love, you may never have shared with each other the important desires you realized you had to abandon for your relationship to work. You may be very reluctant to share those surrendered desires now for fear of threatening your present relationship.

For example, you may have initially loved that your partner was an intensely social person, involved in a multitude of group activities. You loved sharing that life with him because you also had a wonderful intimate life together.

Then, as your relationship matured, his social activities increased, his work involvement deepened, and he was more exhausted when he got home. You were willing and able to accept the balance in your original relationship, but are not happy with how much it has changed. Perhaps your need for quality time has even increased as its availability has lessened. Were you to create a new set of ideals and goals now, you would make those intimate times a higher priority.

Remember, you will only be able to resolve this difference if you are willing to look at what is now truth for each of you. The goal of your healing is to find a new set of common dreams within which both of you can feel authentic and fulfilled.

In the next exercise, promise each other that your goal is to start over without remorse. The past will be more than compensated for by the hope of your new future. Look to what is possible, not to what has been lost.

♥ EXERCISE: Looking at Our Original Ideals and Goals and How We Would Change Them Were We to Meet Now

This exercise has three parts. In this first part, list at least ten ideals and goals you and your partner agreed upon when your love was new. They can be promises you made to each other, ownership of certain material things, or the devotion to common beliefs.

When you have each completed your list, compare the similarities and differences.

Example

1. Having children

2. Living near cultural opportunities

3. Saving most of our money

4. Moving away from family

5. Staying healthy

6. Going to church regularly

7. Both employed

8. No emotional or physical infidelity

9. Being part of the community

10. Keeping our intimacy exciting

The second part of this exercise is to make a list of ten or more common ideals or goals you would now choose if you were starting your relationship over.

Example

1. Traveling

2. Spending more time alone together

3. Spending more time with friends

4. Moving to a rural community

5. Spending more time outdoors

6. Getting rid of stress

7. Learning more together

8. Trying novel things

9. Simplifying life

10. More sex

Share your new lists with each other. See where your new goals and dreams differ from those you originally chose and where they are the same. Do not feel bad if the lists are different. These comparisons are the foundation for creating new dreams and goals that will incorporate what both of you now need and what you may have to willingly relinquish.

In the third part of the exercise, the two of you will place your dreams and goals into three categories:

Category 1: Those that still are the same

Category 2: Those that need negotiating

Category 3: Those that either of you cannot currently
agree upon

Use the following examples as your guide.

Example

Category 1: Same Dreams

More uninterrupted time together

Saving more money

Sharing vulnerabilities

Getting more exercise

Expressing positive feelings

Category 2: Negotiated Dreams

What we eat

Which friends we spend time with

Where we want to travel

How often we make love

What we spend money on

Category 3: Potential Incompatibilities

Religious practices

Political choices

Choice of friends

Acceptable amounts of alcohol use

♥

Suggestions

You may not have perfect agreement on the items in each category or where to place them. That is okay. The goal of the exercise is to see where you began, where you are now, and how you can build your new set of mutual ideals in the future.

You have learned that goals and dreams change and that they must always be open to diverging and reforming. As you contrast, compare, and recommit, listen deeply to each other's reasons for why your ideals may have changed over time.

In going over your lists with your partner, you may be surprised at the different goals and ideals you had at the beginning, and equally so as to what you both want now. You may also learn something unexpected about your partner's level of desire as he or she talks about each item on the list.

Step Three: When Did Your Goals and Ideals Diverge?

So many experiences happen to a couple during their relationship that it is hard to know when their priorities change. Partners who are in love and committed to their relationship often let small differences pass while they focus on the things they cherish. Those small, neglected stumbles can grow into larger ones without the partners realizing it.

For example, new lovers, sincere in their promises, may find that they cannot keep all of them as their relationship matures. Not wanting to disappoint their beloved, they may avoid revealing that they can't live up to those commitments, they may procrastinate, or they may fall into the trap of deluding themselves into thinking they will be able to live up to their promises someday.

Caring partners also want to be fair about using the relationship's resources for something that may not benefit both of them. Yet, despite their good intentions, they may still feel resentful for their sacrifice and consciously or unconsciously be less motivated to grant the personal desires of the other partner.

♥ EXERCISE: When You Started to Change

The goal of this exercise is to recall several situations where you lost interest in a once-shared common goal or dream. There may be many to choose from, but for this exercise, you should select three situations that were meaningful to you both and where diverging from your shared goal significantly affected your relationship.

Write each situation in your journal so that you can share it with your partner later. Use the following directions as your guide:

What was your originally shared goal or dream?

How did you feel when you promised your participation?

What parts of that goal or dream did you and your partner achieve?

How do you feel about it now?

When did your feelings change?

When you knew you felt differently, did you tell your partner?

If yes, how did he or she respond?

Was the response different from what you wanted?

Example

"We'd been together for about a year when you asked me if I would start a small business with you. You wanted your younger brother to get involved in something worthwhile when he finished high school.

"I knew he was into drugs and didn't have much ambition, so I was wary. With both your parents gone, you felt you were the only one who could help him, and I didn't want to let you down. It took all the money I'd saved, and I suspected it would not succeed, but I knew how important it was to you and I'd promised to support your commitments.

"My worst fears were realized when he kept taking money and consistently failed to show up. I knew you felt terrible and tried to make it up by working harder yourself. After two years of our being ripped off, I found a buyer who would take the business off our hands. I needed to stop the negative spiral in a way that wouldn't make you feel guilty about what had happened.

"I reassured you that we gave it our best shot, and that starting the business was my decision as well, but I knew you felt responsible and guilty. I wish now I had talked to you more honestly about it at the time. Maybe if I had, we could have thought of a better way to help your brother. I don't want to get caught up in that kind of thing again. I'm really sorry, baby. I should have shared the way I felt inside."

♥

Suggestions

As you share these memories with your partner, stay away from assigning blame or invalidating your individual recollections. In learning new and tender things about each other, you will be better able to share your future dreams without hiding your intentions.

Step Four: What Could You Have Done When Your Goals and Dreams Began Diverging?

Goals and dreams rarely change overnight. What may seem desirable at one time can become uninteresting at another. These unpredictable shifts can undermine your commitment to each other.

For legitimate reasons, you may have waited before complaining, or you might have doubted your own internal changes. Perhaps one of you may have tried to communicate your feelings, but the other partner was resistant. Or, maybe one of you decided to pursue a different goal without telling the other, downplaying its importance so it would be less threatening.

Any of these non-sharing tactics can seem right in the moment, but they mask a growing difference that might have been resolved had you addressed it earlier.

♥ EXERCISE: Changing Your Goals Without Sharing Your Decision with Your Partner

In your journal, write memories of three times when you supported one of your partner's goals or dreams but didn't tell your partner when your feelings changed and you were no longer on board.

As you write your memories, let these following questions guide your answers:

1. What was your original shared goal or dream?

2. When did you know you no longer felt the same way?

3. Why did you not tell your partner your feelings had changed?

4. What did you wish could have happened?

5. What did you do instead?

6. What eventually happened?

7. How do you feel now about what you chose to do?

Using these questions as a guide, write a narrative to your partner about what happened. These revelations can be any length; what's important is that you open your heart and share what was really going on with you.

Example

"This is one of the hardest things I've ever done. It's painful enough to remember the choices I made, but even more so to tell you now. I want to feel close to you again, and I'm willing to do whatever it takes, so let me do this exercise the best I can.

"Before we made a commitment to each other, you told me very clearly that you didn't want to recreate your parents' loveless marriage. Your dad traveled all the time, and when your parents were together, they had little to talk about. We promised each other that nothing would ever be more important than our relationship.

"I never expected to become so successful so soon. I hadn't set my sights that high as a kid, and when the cases came in so fast and our income soared, I got caught up in being important for the first time in my life. I know I started to spend more time at the office and broke a lot of dates with you, sometimes at the last minute.

"You kept asking me if I'd changed my priorities and I told you that I hadn't, that this pace would slow down eventually. I promised compensatory time, and then never delivered.

"I had my secretary send roses and notes of further promises. I could see your heart breaking, but I just couldn't give up my passion for what I was doing. I wanted to renegotiate our original commitments, but I didn't know how to make that happen without your feeling cheated. I would have loved it if you'd taken more of an interest in my world, but I couldn't seem to interest you in doing that. Instead of trying to work it out with you, I just kept promising the situation would change someday.

"I remember the night I came home late again and you were gone. I couldn't imagine life without you, but I knew I deserved it. I agonized for every minute of the three months it took to convince you to come back.

"I know we've recreated our new dreams together and we're better, but somehow I don't think our relationship has ever fully recovered. I'm so incredibly sorry for not telling you what was really going on and for putting you through this."

♥

Suggestions

This is the part of healing where you're going to share the times in your life when you internally betrayed your partner but didn't share what you were feeling. These confessions are difficult to make and often hard to hear. Sometimes they can bring up sad or angry feelings, and you will need to find forgiveness to move on. Surprisingly, some will bring unexpected tender and meaningful feelings instead.

Stay kind and considerate. Do not let feelings of blame or resentment creep in. Your goal in these exercises is to lay the foundation for a stumble-proof relationship in the future.

Step Five: What Do You Need from Each Other Now to Rebuild Your Common Goals?

Remember, you committed to your mutual goals, ideals, and dreams willingly with love and hope. Because some ideals have diminished and others have taken their place, you may feel somewhat overwhelmed and not know quite how to repair things.

This is the time to be honest and realize that you know each other much better now. You can make more successful choices about future common goals and dreams, and you can count on being able to deliver in the future.

Open communication and the willingness to reshape the common goals and dreams of a relationship are crucial to its continuing success. The more flexible and creative a couple can be, the more hope and joy they can find in their new, mutually chosen direction.

♥ EXERCISE: Ten Sacred Goals

In this exercise, you and your partner will list your new mutual goals and dreams. These will be commitments you both feel are sacred, ones that cannot be broken without renegotiating with your partner. You must also promise each other that you'll be open and flexible when you reveal yourself. It is crucial that your communication stays open and your commitments are continuously updated.

Your written examples must consist of agreements you know you can, and will, keep. Open your hearts to each other, keeping all of your feelings current and shared.

In your journal, write ten goals for you and your partner that you feel will help you heal any separation between you. Write them in detail so they are clear. Your partner will do the same. The items you each list can be achievements, possessions, attitudes, behaviors, or commitments to outside interests, but they must be important to you.

When you compare your lists, you will hopefully end up with at least five that overlap. They will form the beginning of many more as you discover them throughout your life together.

The example below is to help guide you. Your lists will consist of those goals that are personal to your own relationship.

Example

1. I want us to pay off our debts and stay financially solvent.

2. I want us both to commit to do whatever we need to stay healthy.

3. I want us to stay sexually faithful to each other and do whatever we need to maintain our passion.

4. I want us to find a path to a God we can both embrace and worship together.

5. I want us to spend at least one prime-time hour every week just with each other, remembering the blessings that we have together.

6. I want us to give more time to helping others less fortunate.

7. I want us to keep making efforts to interest each other in new experiences.

8. I want us to be open about our sorrows and fears.

9. I want us to live more simply and acquire less.

10. I want us to make each other our first priority and agree before we choose others.

♥

Suggestions

As you share your dreams, you are likely to feel vulnerable and concerned about your partner's acceptance and agreement. This is a natural part of the process. Don't judge each other's choices or feel disappointed if you don't always agree.

Comparing your lists will help you to know each other's most important goals and desires. In your open and honest sharing, you can choose to throw entries out, add new ones, or change them in any way you want. Until you are comfortable in continuously updating each other, do this exercise regularly to stay on track.

Step Six: Keeping the Same Dreams

If you've done the exercises in sequence in this chapter, you're already well on your way to creating common goals and dreams for the rest of your relationship.

Let's assume your process has been wonderfully effective, your hearts are beating as one again, and you know yourselves well enough to not promise what you can't deliver. What do you need to know now to stay on track?

Many times couples have the best of intentions and yet forget to watch over their interactions. They allow the same drifting that got them in trouble before. They are completely motivated to do things better, yet fail because of unpredictable events, or the all-too-human laziness that can seduce us all.

This is the time to look once more at your own behavior. In this last exercise, you're going to recall the times in the past where your good intentions have fallen by the wayside and examine why that happened.

♥ EXERCISE: What I Need to Watch for in My Own Behavior

In your journal, write memories of three times when you let other priorities divert you from commitments you had made to another person. The goal is to make you aware of the behaviors you have to watch so that you can make better decisions in the future.

We all have had embarrassing moments when we let someone down. Having compassion for our own humanness can help us to forgive it in others.

In writing these examples down, look for what got in the way of your commitment and why you chose to do what you did instead. Ask yourself if those recurring rationalizations have a common theme you can watch for in the future. At what point did you become aware that you were going to break your commitment?

Using these questions as a guide, write a narrative to share with your partner. Your confession can be about something between you and your partner or from an earlier time in your life unrelated to your current relationship.

Example

"This is really uncomfortable, because I don't have to look very far to remember letting someone down. The first one that comes to mind was promising my high school weightlifting team that I'd add extra workouts every day to help us win the title that year.

"What they didn't know is that I was newly in love with a gorgeous girl who had offered to be my first sexual partner. We probably had sex twice a day for a month. I'd never felt so great. It got way too easy to forget everything else.

"Needless to say, I didn't hit the gym much, but I didn't tell my team. On the day of the meet, I sucked. I think I pretended that I had the flu or something, but they knew I had flaked on them. I felt terrible. I knew what I was doing the whole time and chose to do what I wanted instead of what I had promised.

"It would have been tough to do, but I should have either kept my word or quit the team when I knew I couldn't live up to my promise. At least they would have had time to find someone else. That memory has haunted me ever since."

Example

"I asked my dad to loan me some money to start investing. I knew he didn't have much, but he always backed me, no matter what.

"I did okay at first, but then those skis were on sale and I convinced myself I really needed them. That started the change of direction, but I never told my dad. When he found out, I knew I'd irreversibly damaged his trust in me.

"I should have let the skis stay where they were and done what I promised I'd do. If I'd made the money I should have, I could have gotten them later and not hurt my dad."

Common Theme: Getting carried away with something self-indulgent that I can't stay away from, even when I know I'm making the wrong decision.

♥

Suggestions

The more examples you can find, the better you'll get at realizing how your good intentions can be sabotaged by emerging priorities. Ask your partner to help you recognize them in your relationship or with other people, before they can sabotage your new intentions.

Go over the commitments you've made to each other and make certain they are still viable, top priorities. If you want to stay open to each other, you will need to practice humility and the willingness to be vulnerable. That process is healing in and of itself.

Reflections

Common goals and dreams form the foundation of trust in the present and faith in the future. In every relationship, they will transform over time as a result of a couple's resources and their challenges.

At any one time, both partners must be willing to commit their deepest reverence and loyalty, not only to each other, but to the values they hold in common.

You can have the security of that kind of sacred place together if you are willing to communicate what is important to you and listen deeply to the same from your partner. Even the new goals and dreams you are building together now are likely to change as your relationship evolves. Stay in constant touch with each other's feelings and desires, practice your flexibility, and remind one other to be open to future transformations when the opportunity arises.

creating a
stumble-proof future

"Let's never lose each other again."

Every intimate relationship is susceptible to stumbling. New lovers are vigilant in their watchfulness over each other's needs and dreams, but as their relationship develops, they can fall prey to choosing other priorities that can undermine those early commitments.

Concerned that being totally honest with each other might threaten the good connections that are still intact, you may have pretended stumbles were not happening or minimized their importance. Or, having only so much time and energy to devote to each other and to life's demands, you might not have even noticed them. As time went by and there was no resolution, your stumbles took hold and began to undermine what once was a beautiful love.

You must be aware of discernible warning signs that can help expose potential stumbles before they threaten your love for each other. With awareness and humility, you can heal your mistakes and keep from stumbling again.

The Warning Signs

The warning signs of a stumble can be hard to identify in the midst of your relationship's ups and downs. But if you are aware of their potential, you can recognize them by their common symptoms and distressing effects.

Whichever stumbles apply to your relationship, you will know one is happening if you feel that you are emotionally, physically, or spiritually growing apart.

Stumbles can make your disconnects more frequent and harder to resolve. They can also leave unresolved sorrow in their wake, creating emotional barriers that may be hard to overcome. Even after you have reconnected, your intimate interactions may not fully bring back the closeness you once shared.

Denial as the Enemy

Because you've wanted your relationship to survive, you may have ignored the signals that told you something was going wrong and focused instead on those that were still working. Perhaps you hoped that any significant problems, even when increasing in intensity and frequency, were just bumps in the road. It may have been easier to push your problems aside rather than face them. You may have even attempted to expose the problems between you in the past and felt it made the situation worse, so you are reticent to take that chance again.

Denial is the most common yet most potentially destructive response to a beginning stumble. It is the number one enemy of problem resolution. As the pressure of the problem builds, the need to strengthen denial must increase, and the more the problem is ignored, the more likely it will become more serious later on.

When Denial Is No Longer Possible

When your stumbles can no longer be ignored and you are forced to awaken from your denial, you have four options. They range from superficial and temporary resolutions to transformative change. It may seem easier and less challenging to choose a temporary solution, but the stumble will return, and usually with greater intensity.

Options for Resolution

1. You can agree to postpone dealing with your stumble, though you both know it is not a permanent resolution. You agree that you do not have the time or energy to deal with it in the present, and you commit to working on it sometime in the future.

2. You can deal with the problem superficially and pretend to each other that there has been resolution when there clearly has not. This secondary denial will eventually increase the severity of the problem.

3. You can minimize the problem and focus on what is still good in your relationship, hoping your positive connections will eclipse the issue and eventually render it powerless. Though that may be possible, it is unlikely. More often the suppressed stumble begins to undermine what is good in the relationship as well.

4. You can choose to be absolutely honest about how you feel and what you are experiencing, creating a plan to work at resolving the issue that is driving you apart. You become genuine friends to each other again, open to doing whatever you need to do to begin healing the distance between you.

In the first three options, you are unfortunately still being seduced by denial, just in a different form. Those redefinitions of the problem may delude you into believing that they will not threaten the core of your relationship. That is a dangerous assumption. If the stumble is significant and you continue to deny it, you are facing an emergent catastrophe.

Only option number four can promote the necessary healing you are seeking. If you use your tools to heal the stumble at its inception, you can not only keep it from doing damage, but identify others that may be connected.

♥ EXERCISE: How to Recognize Potentially Destructive Denial

The following questions will help you identify destructive denial. Score your answers according to these options:

> I share my concerns with my partner immediately = 1
>
> I usually wait a while, in hopes things will change = 2
>
> I tend to not want to rock the boat when other areas are going well = 3
>
> I avoid the conflict because I'm concerned it will get out of hand = 4
>
> I suppress my discomfort because it's easier than causing a problem = 5
>
> I talk myself out of my unhappiness = 6

1. When I feel afraid that my partner is losing interest sexually, _____ .

2. When we seem to be arguing more about unimportant things, _____ .

3. When my partner seems to care for himself or herself more than me, _____ .

4. When I'm upset that my partner would rather do things separately, _____ .

5. When my partner and I don't see eye to eye on something important, _____ .

6. When my partner doesn't seem interested in my concerns, _____ .

7. When I feel that we are not enjoying the same things as much anymore, _____ .

8. When it takes us much longer to get over arguments, _____ .

9. When my partner seems preoccupied and unavailable much of the time, _____ .

10. When my partner doesn't seek me out to share his or her life, _____ .

Scoring

Add up your individual scores. A score of 20 or under means that you are facing your issues and not allowing denial to derail you. If you score from 21 to 40, you're carefully selecting what seems okay to share. If those decisions are working, and you're not creating a growing disconnect underneath, you may be okay. If your score is 41 or above, whether you are aware of it or not, you are withdrawing from your partner.

If your score is very different from your partner's, go over each of the questions together and observe the differences. Use them to create your healing plan.

♥

Unconscious Denial

Some stumbles are so intertwined with the positive parts of your relationship, or so threatening, that you may not have been able to recognize when one had started. You may have sensed that something wasn't right yet were unable to put your finger on what was happening.

When you are denying an experience that you are not ready or able to recognize, you may only be able to detect it by observing your physical and emotional changes. An underlying stumble may not be obvious, but if you are willing to look closely at those symptoms and search deeply for what they represent, you will see the underlying invisible stumble that is causing them.

In the following sections, you will be reintroduced to each of the stumbles you've read about, along with some of the more common symptoms of unconscious denial that accompany each one. Your own symptoms may be similar to or different from those presented here. Use this list of steps as your guide for finding what stumbles you might be experiencing:

1. Title a journal entry with the stumble you are exploring.

2. List any symptoms you recognize in yourself that may signal unconscious emotional and physical responses to that stumble.

3. Evaluate how often each symptom occurs and how severe it is.

4. Does this stumble apply to you?

5. If so, bring the stumble into your conscious awareness so that you and your partner may work together to find the intimacy you've lost.

Common Symptoms of Unconscious Denial

Some of the unconscious symptoms can overlap with those of other stumbles as well, and your partner may experience different symptoms while enduring the same stumble. Your goal is to bring each of your unconscious experiences to the surface by asking yourselves what underlying problems these symptoms represent.

Use these examples to share your feelings with your partner. You may be able to do that more effectively by comparing what you are experiencing now with what you have felt in the past when your intimacy was more intact. If your symptoms can be recognized and resolved, you will be able to recover your mutual honest devotion.

Stumble: Disillusionment

All partners in relationships will disappoint each other from time to time. Most of these emotional setbacks are unintentional. The partners in healthy relationships learn from them, plan differently for future interactions, and usually move on with little residual damage.

But if disappointments increase in intensity and duration, one or both partners may begin to feel betrayed and disillusioned. They didn't see the stumble begin, and now they have seriously damaged their trust in each other's promises.

Common symptoms of increasing disappointments:

- Mistrust

- Withdrawal

- Lack of faith in new promises

- Feeling like a fool

- Bitterness

Stumble: Boredom

If you have become bored in your intimate partnership, your partner probably is as well. You may still share moments of spontaneous excitement that both of you treasure, but they have lessened in duration and frequency.

Many couples feel that the diminished excitement between them is a normal part of a long-term relationship. They do not recognize that it might be an underlying warning sign of something more significant.

Common symptoms of boredom:

- Feeling trapped

- Picking fights

- Finding fault

- Fantasizing about other potential partners
- Feeling flat and uninspired

Stumble: Destructive Conflicts

Debates can be exciting and productive differences of opinion and experience. Blow a mental whistle and you should be able to represent either side with the same enthusiasm and purpose.

On the other hand, arguments to establish dominance are not healthy. If you win, your partner loses, or vice versa. You will become temporary competitive enemies and your intimacy will diminish. If the stumble continues, those losses will increase.

Common symptoms of destructive conflicts:

- Irritability
- Reactivity
- Resistance to influence or control
- Quickness to anger and blame
- Focusing on the differences between you rather than the similarities

Stumble: Self-Preservation

The person you would have risked your life for before now seems woefully less important to you than yourself. After many interactions where you expected your partner to take care of you and then instead had to take care of your own needs, you may have lost confidence that your gifts will be fairly reciprocated. Or you may have just promised too much sacrifice at the beginning of your relationship and can't meet your own commitments any longer.

However that imbalance may have occurred, you're in a self-preservation mode now, and you feel that your relationship isn't going in the right direction.

Common symptoms of self-preservation:

- Righteousness
- Self-pity
- Hurt
- Isolation
- Resentment

Stumble: Operating Solo

You used to do everything together and only go your separate ways when you both agreed it was okay. The two of you together were an incredible team, more than the sum of your parts. What you couldn't handle well, your partner could. You were like musketeers, covering each other's backs and working on challenges together.

Now, you find yourself avoiding even asking for your partner's participation, let alone depending on him or her when you need help.

Common symptoms of operating solo:

- Toughening up
- Feeling separate
- Not expecting help
- Uninterested in your partner's input
- Brooding

Stumble: Loss of Unconditional Love

You've lost your symbolic haven and no longer feel automatically welcome in the arms of your partner. You're still devoted to the relationship, but you don't feel the same automatic support you once cherished and felt entitled to.

You know your original expectations were colored by the passion of new love. You would like to recreate a new safe haven that both of you can count on again, but you don't know how to find your way back. You're feeling lost and in love at the same time.

Common symptoms of missing your safe haven:

- Feeling abandoned

- A deep sadness

- Insecurity

- Trying to be brave

- Feeling on trial

Stumble: Outside Interests

You've exhausted the resources within your relationship that used to keep you entranced. You're desperately seeking interesting things you can still do together, but you don't feel your partner is cooperating.

Though you may still treasure certain aspects of your connection, you more often find yourself looking elsewhere to feel alive again. You would rather find those special moments with your partner, but whatever you've done doesn't seem to be helping.

Common symptoms of focusing on outside interests:

- Loneliness

- Conflict

- Dissatisfaction

- Discouragement

- Resentment

Stumble: Different Dreams

You began your relationship intertwined in the same dreams and goals. Now you somehow feel less connected, concerned that you are going in different directions in areas that seem crucial. You want to agree again about what is mutually important, but can't seem to share how you feel or understand your partner's behavior.

It is natural for each partner to have some separate goals as the relationship matures. When their relationship is still their highest priority, they make certain that outside interests bring energy back into their interactions rather than steal resources from their devotion to each other.

When their common goals and dreams appear to be dangerously diverging, the partners must recommit to creating new ones that can include each of their personal transformations.

Common symptoms of diverging dreams and goals:

- An aching sense of separateness

- Worries about loss of connection

- Disillusionment

- Feeling adrift

- Feeling grief without a clear reason

As these symptoms challenge your mutual devotion, you can lose your intimate connection without realizing it. By identifying the symptoms that may be unconscious warnings of emotional disconnection, you can identify and repair your stumbles.

Can you imagine a relationship where you and your partner become aware of your stumbles as soon as they begin and have the skills and motivation to immediately heal them? If you could catch them at their inception, you would never again have to deal with the heartbreaking residue they create. Over time they would rarely reoccur, and if they did, you would use them to deepen your commitment to each other.

If you have completed your exercises and internalized the lessons they contain, you are ready to commit to a new kind of relationship, one where you:

- Are supportive of each other's dreams and ideas

- Live in each other's hearts

- Feel connected and deeply interested in the relationship

- Know for certain that both of you want to stay together

- Are comfortable in each other's chosen dependence or interdependence

- Are open to challenge and change

- Are non-reactive and resilient

- Are confident in your ability to face life's challenges together

Reflections and Conclusions

New love is filled with mystery, magnetic attraction, and astonishing resilience. The partners in a blossoming relationship enthusiastically try to fulfill each other's dreams, lovingly challenge each other's inconsistencies, and readily forgive misunderstandings and errors. They focus intensely on one another physically, sexually, mentally, and emotionally, and provide a guaranteed secure haven where either partner is always welcome to come for regeneration and support.

As all relationships mature, couples transform from a pleasure seeking, excited, generous team to become two individuals who develop new interests and different priorities that may pull them away from each other. As they incorporate those other priorities, they may feel their love begin to waver.

When that happens, stumbles can endanger a previously secure relationship. If the partners do not attend to the initial warnings, they can find themselves drifting apart in areas crucial to the relationship's long-term survival.

Any relationship is prone to stumbles. Aware, committed partners help each other when they begin to fall. They not only stay together but get closer through resolving their problems. When their love is threatened, they immediately focus on their relationship as their first priority and commit to its healing and regeneration. Given even a reasonable chance, love can always find its way home.

suggested reading

Bugental, James F. T. 1999. *Psychotherapy Isn't What You Think.* Redding, CT: Zeig, Tucker, and Theisen.

Gottleib, Lori. 2010. *Marry Him: The Case for Settling for Mr. Good Enough.* New York: Dutton Adult.

Gottman, John M. and Nan Silver. 2000. *The Seven Principles That Make Marriage Work.* New York: The Crown Publishing Group.

Gunther, Randi. 2010. *Relationship Saboteurs: The Ten Behaviors That Undermine Love.* Oakland, CA: New Harbinger Publications.

Harris, Russ. 1999. *Act with Love.* Oakland, CA: New Harbinger Publications.

Hendrix, Harville. 2008. *Getting the Love You Want.* New York: Henry Holt & Company.

McKay, Matthew, Patrick Fanning, and Kim Paleg. 2006. *Couple Skills: Making Your Relationship Work.* 2nd ed. Oakland, CA: New Harbinger Publications.

Peck, Scott and Shannon. 2006. *Love Skills for Personal and Global Transformation.* Marin County, CA: Life Path.

Ruiz, Don Miguel. 1997. *The Four Agreements: A Practical Guide to Personal Freedom.* San Rafael, CA: Amber-Allen.

Siegel, Judith. 2010. *Stop Overreacting: Effective Strategies for Calming Your Emotions.* Oakland, CA: New Harbinger Publications.

Valentine, Mary and John. 2003. *Romantic Intelligence.* Oakland, CA: New Harbinger Publications.

Randi Gunther, PhD, is a clinical psychologist and marriage counselor in Lomita, CA. She has given multiple workshops and lectures, inspiring hundreds of couples to go beyond their limitations to create successful relationships. A practical idealist, she encourages couples to give up their deadlocked limitations and pursue the freedom to find new purpose together. In more than forty years of practice, she has spent over 90,000 face-to-face hours helping individuals and couples.